Finding Peace of Mind

SPIRITUALITY FOR A GLOBAL WORLD

VOLUME II

Finding Peace of Mind

SPIRITUALITY FOR A GLOBAL WORLD

VOLUME I

Select Writings of

J. P. VASWANI

Compiled and Edited with an Introduction by
Anita Raina Thapan

FULL CIRCLE

FIND PEACE OF MIND

First Paperback Edition, 2011
ISBN 978-81-7621-226-7

Published by **FULL CIRCLE** *PUBLISHING*
J-40, Jorbagh Lane, New Delhi-110003
Tel: 011-24620063, 24621011 • Fax: 24645795
E-mail: contact@fullcirclebooks.in • *website:* www.fullcirclebooks.in

Designing & Typesetting : SCANSET
J-40, Jorbagh Lane, New Delhi-110003

Printed at Yash Printographics, B-123, Sector-10, Noida-201301

PRINTED IN INDIA
11/11/01/12/33/SCANSET/DE/YP/YP/NP300/NP300

CONTENTS

FOREWORD

"Life has no meaning," said a young man to me. He is highly educated and is a popular Professor at the University.

Sometimes, when we are sitting in silence, a voice within us asks: "What for am I here?" "Who am I?" "How can I make a difference?" From where have I come?" "Whither am I moving?"

Three centuries ago, the poet John Dryden said: "Every age has a kind of universal genius, which inclines those that live in it to some particular studies."

The twentieth century produced Albert Einstein who had a genius for exploring the material world. People travelled in space, walked on the moon, invented gadgets that could perform miracles. The early years of the twenty-first century have revealed that there is something more than knowledge of the physical world – and that is spirituality.

It is commonly believed that a spiritual man is even he who turns away from the world or who lives a life of isolation and solitude. Far from it, spiritual life is all inclusive: to be truly spiritual is not to live for self alone: it is to see oneself in all – men and birds and animals, fish and fowl, indeed in every atom.

Is this not the essence of Vedanta – that all life is One, and that the spirit of God permeates the entire Universe?

I am not one of those who believe that spirituality has no

place, no relevance in today's world. Quite to the contrary, I firmly believe that there is a spiritual renaissance that is happening all around us. More and more people are beginning to realize that money, material comforts, power and satisfaction of sense-desires cannot bring them what they need most – peace, contentment and inner harmony.

At a question and answer session in a public forum, a youngster once asked me: "Dada, why is it that all our saints and sages say the same thing? And why do they say the same things over and over again?"

I replied, "When they are convinced that what they have to say has been absorbed by us, they will move on to different things. But can we give them the assurance that we have understood and assimilated the truths that they teach?"

Let us put ourselves to the test: how many of us can honestly say that we have absorbed, assimilated and put into practice the following ideals?

- Satyam vada krodham makuru
- Satyameva jayate
- Do unto others what you would have others do unto you.
- Love thy neighbours
- Do not covet what does not belong to you.
- Speak gently to everyone
- Treat everyone you meet with kindness and courtesy.

Let us admit – we have not even touched upon 'higher' ideals such as Oneness of all Life, awareness of the spirit or even recognition of the Supreme Being.

More often than not, when I touch upon such values as honesty, truth and integrity, kind friends tell me that I am being unworldly, for I am not aware of the realities of the Global marketplace.

They add, for my benefit, that values and ethics 'have their place' somewhere in theory on principle, but cannot be out into practice, for it will only ruin their business interests.

Do you now begin to see why our saints and sages have to keep repeating themselves? And why little ones like me are still at work, drawing the attention of my fellow travelers on the road of life – my fellow pilgrims, if I may use that word – to spiritual: deeds and aspirations.

In this task, I am grateful that I have the benefit of friends like Ms Anita Raina Thapan, who has taken it upon herself to carry my humble words to a wider audience.

We, at the Sadhu Vaswani Mission, had the privilege of coming into contact with Anita in the Dada Darshan project that has indeed been a dream of ours for the last two decades. Anita was sensitive, discerning and perceptive: she has ability, intelligence and a maverick creativity. Her heart, mind and soul were obviously touched by what she heard and read of the Master, Gurudev Sadhu Vaswani. Out of this first impression aroused her decision to bring out a book compiling same of my writings.

I express my appreciation for her sensitivity and understanding of the Master's ideals. She is a wonderful human being blessed with those qualities of head, hand and heart that have made her so receptive; and that is more important to store what she had seen and read with others.

Anita has said certain things about me in her gracious introduction which I have done little to deserve. But whatever good she has seen in me, whichever of my writings she has chosen to publish, all that I know and say, I have learnt at the feet of my Gurudev. All glory to the Master!

A lecturer preached about the immensity of God, urging that God is everywhere. He noticed that when he said these words a little shepherd girl shows signs of great joy. When the lecture was over he called the girl and asked her why she had been so happy. She replied immediately: "Because from now on I will not be afraid any longer when I am alone, in the forest tending the flock. I was afraid because I was afraid I was alone: but now I will know that the Lord is with me."

"Yes," said the lecturer, "You are not alone, God is there, but you may not see him with your physical eyes."

"That doesn't matter," said the girl, "As long as I know He is there! At night I used to be afraid to sleep alone, but then I realized my sister was with me. I can't see her in the darkness, but it's enough for me to know she is there. The same thing will happen in the woods. I know the Lord is there and although I may not see Him, I will no longer be afraid because I will not be alone."

The little shepherd girl was spiritual. She had taken the first step. She realized she was not alone. When shall we take the first step?

– J. P. Vaswani

INTRODUCTION

Dada J.P. Vaswami (1918)

Jashan Pahlajrai Vaswani, known to his devotees as Dada Jashan, is the nephew of Sadhu Vaswani. Born on August 2, 1918, in Hyderabad, Sind, J.P. Vaswani was the first son of Pahlajrai, the beloved elder brother of Sadhu Vaswani. At the time, Pahlajrai was working at the Hyderabad Training College for Teachers. He eventually rose to the position of Supervisor of Municipal Schools. Unlike many of his contemporaries, Pahlajrai could speak and write English well. Young Vaswani's mother, Krishnadevi, had also received a little English education. Gifted with a wonderful intellect and an open-mind, she had the courage to break with the tradition of her day, replacing the traditional long skirts of Sindhi women with the sari. She also refused to cover her face, as was customary for Sindhi women of that time.

Young Vaswani displayed exceptional intelligence and capability at school from a tender age and completed his primary education in three years instead of the usual five. The sudden death of his father while he was in high school suddenly plunged the family into a severe financial crisis and motivated his courageous mother to become a teacher. This was a pioneering step as she became one of the earliest Sindhi women to take up a profession. While she strove to support her family of five children, she pinned her future hopes on her eldest son, Jashan, who consistently produced brilliant results in school, and later in college.

At thirteen, young Jashan joined the D. J. Sind college, Karachi, for a graduation degree in science. Standing first in the University he became a Fellow of the College. The family and well-wishers were confident that the young man would easily qualify for the Indian Civil Service. That, however, was not to be for, as he grew, all ambition vanished in the young man. Instead, he felt irresistibly drawn to his uncle and future Master, Sadhu Vaswani. At the insistence of the latter, however, young Vaswani completed his M.Sc. in Physics. His thesis entitled *The Scattering of X-rays by Solids* was assessed by none other than Sir C.V. Raman, the future Nobel Laureate. Thereafter, young Vaswani was offered the post of lecturer. But the pull of his uncle and Master was greater. Finally, his reluctant mother, seeing that he would only be happy following his heart, blessed him and let him go. Thus began a life-long relationship of disciple and Master.

When J. P. Vaswani was born, Sadhu Vaswani had been the Principal of the prestigious Mahendra College, Patiala. His visits to Hyderabad took place only during the holidays. However, in 1929 when Sadhu Vaswani came to live in Hyderabad, his contact with his three nephews and two nieces became a regular feature of their lives. Sadhu Vaswani's visits to the home were always eagerly looked forward to by the children. He would narrate to them stories from the lives of the great ones of East and West and also play with them. But from an early age, there seemed to be a special bond between the Uncle and young Jashan. Many of the latter's childhood experiences with his uncle left an indelible impression in the young child's mind. He reminisces: "we were little ones and he used to be like a little one among little ones. And we were always sure of him. We knew that if we had a grievance we had only to report it and he would take our side. We were always sure of that. We used to wait for his coming. He used to come every evening. We used to wait and if we had any complaint then we knew that now our chance has come."

As a young boy, Jashan Vaswani displayed many traits of character similar to his uncle. He showed a marked inclination to spend long moments in silence and reflection. A voracious reader, he was inspired by his father and uncle, both brilliant orators, to try his hand at public speaking. At eight he won his first prize in an elocution competition and discovered that public speaking came to him very naturally. His English was flawless and he had a prodigious memory.

Deeply influenced by his Uncle who had spent considerable time wandering and living in the villages of Sind after resigning from professional life, the young teenager, Jashan, also went, many a time, on his own to the villages of Sind, in quiet retreat without carrying any luggage and trusting himself wholly to the loving care of God. Often he slept under a tree and ate a common meal at the zamindar's *langar*. On such occasions he would sometimes come into contact with saints and men of God.

The young man grew into an intellectual who had a voracious appetite for books. Besides being highly perceptive, he also had a logical and analytical mind that questioned, rather than blindly accepted anything he was told. Because of this, his early days of discipleship were given to many an argument and debate with his Master. But young Vaswani had the special privilege of living with his Master. He was able to watch him waking, eating, working, dreaming, sleeping, serving, chanting, meditating, ever-loving – denying himself to none! And thus the disciple was moulded into the likeness of his Master. Dada Jashan later made it explicit that once a spiritual aspirant has set his foot firmly on the Path, he must channelize all his energies exclusively to serving the master in every way possible. By attuning himself to the needs of the guru, the disciple opens the door of receptivity to the divine grace that flows to every sincere disciple.

Over time, the questioning spirit that had dominated the early phase of J.P. Vaswani's spiritual growth, gave way to a phase of absolute and complete acceptance. There came the day when he saw life through the eyes of his Master. He recalls an incident: "One afternoon it was 12 o'clock and Sadhu Vaswani said "I want to go down to the hall." So we brought a chair. He used to be carried in a chair and we brought him down. And there he sat and dozed off. When he got up he asked what the time was. I told him it was 12 o'clock. He asked whether it was 12 o'clock during the day or during the night. I replied that it was 12 o'clock during the day. He said, no, its 12 o'clock at night, its midnight. I said, it must be so if you say so. He said go and see outside and then come and report to me. So I went out and I actually – this is something which you may not believe – I actually went and saw, the sky was dark, the stars were shining and I came and reported it to him. I said it is indeed midnight. And after a little while, the inquisitive person that I am, I thought how did this happen at all? So, once again, I went out and I saw that it was actually day. But his saying had such an effect on me, or whatever it is, that I actually, I actually, I'm telling you, I saw stars. But that was a great day in my life when I realized that whatever the Master says, he's right." The great spiritual link between Master and disciple is most poignantly captured in a poem that Sadhu Vaswani wrote for Dada Jashan entitled "Child of my Tears". In it, he refers to Dada Jashan as the "child of my tears and prayers", as the "child of my destiny."

There are many parallels between Master and Disciple. Their lives are like one flowing river whose waters are a perennial source of spiritual energy and healing. Dada Jashan has been gifted with the same erudition, blessed with the same power of the pen and of speech as his Master was. Like Sadhu Vaswani before him, he is the embodiment of humility and gentleness. In him, like in his mentor, academic excellence has been blended with profound spiritual insight. Even as Sadhu Vaswani took the pen name Nuri for his mystical outpourings of poetry, so has Dada J.P. Vaswani taken the pen-name Anjali. From both their mouths has gushed a stream of sacred poetry, the spontaneous expression of a heart overflowing with love, reveling in supreme bliss.

Often, in the midst of nature, or sometimes even suddenly when in ecstasy, Dada Jashan's eyes close, his fingers beat a rhythm against his knuckles and from his lips flow song after song, full of longing and love, of joy and peace, of adoration and sympathy. Devotees who are around, immediately note down the words on slips of paper. Many of these songs in Sindhi have been gathered together and today form a huge compilation.

When Sadhu Vaswani was confined to bed from 1960-1966, his weak state of health made it impossible for him to personally meet the hundreds who flocked to see him everyday. And so, it was up to the disciple to undertake the Master's responsibility. When the Master passed away, the mantle fell to the shoulders of Dada J.P. Vaswani. He strives, in the true spirit of the Master, to carry far and wide the message of his Master, to dispel gloom and darkness in the hearts of men and to spread the sunshine of hope and joy wherever he goes.

J.P. Vaswani's Message to the World

Dada Jashan seeks to awaken love in the hearts of fellow men and fill them with inner peace. This is the urgent need of the day, for how can modern man find a solution to the wars and violence that tear our world apart, when he does not have peace within himself? The key to peace, says Dada Jashan, is kindness towards all living things. Today we use gun-control as a means of protection for public leaders and private citizens. But here again, protection, as well as peace, does not depend upon outer things. Gun-control laws, which, no doubt, are desperately needed, cannot reach the inner spirit of man, particularly when his soul is confined in a body poisoned by embalmed foods, alcoholic drinks, and hallucinatory drugs. Brought up in a climate of physical, mental and moral decay, contemporary man is incapable of bringing about the change that is so urgently needed in this strife-torn world of ours. Only a new kind of individual can hope to accomplish this. Dada Jashan seeks to awaken that noble individual who slumbers within each one of us.

Man is essentially a spiritual being. Without an awareness of the spiritual dimension of his being, he lives at the mere physical level unable to lift his mind and consciousness to that noble state from which alone he can usher in an era of peace and goodwill between all men and between man and his environment. It is not political leaders, treaties and constitutions that can usher in change. The violent forces that have received an impetus through modern literature, science, music and art can only be controlled and solved individually by each man, woman and child. No laws can reform societies, for societies are made up of individuals and each individual is unique. It is through personal effort and inspiration that individuals transform. And it is only transformed individuals who can inspire transformation in others. Any reading of history shows that the greatest of kings and reformers have eventually been relegated to the dustbin of history. The only names that continue to inspire reverence, centuries after their exit from this world, are those of spiritual masters such as Jesus and Buddha, Krishna and Mohammad and other such spiritual figures who have walked this earth from time to time. The world's greatest movements of thought and action have invariably flowed from the work of a single man.

Sadhu Vaswani and his disciple, Dada Jashan, belong to the category of men whose lives have been poured out as sacrifice on the altar of humanity. When in 1984 Dada Jashan was invited to speak on 'Universal Peace' at the Dag Hammarsjold auditorium of the UN, he declared: "Even if all the statesmen signed a declaration of peace, we would not have peace. Peace does not depend on governments. There can be no peace in the world as long as the hearts of men are a volcano. Even if the governments were to ban the bomb, it would not lead to peace. For the bomb is only a symptom of the disease. We must treat the cause. So long as selfishness and hatred exist in the hearts of men, so long will wars continue to mutilate humanity. Therefore, if you would have peace, begin with the child."

He has also repeatedly emphasized that: "wars will not cease until all killing is stopped. No sentient creature must be killed. For if a man kills an animal for food, he will not hesitate in killing a fellow-man whom he regards as an enemy. We must grow in the spirit of reverence for all life. All life must be regarded as sacred."

Dada Jashan brings with him an air of tranquility and serenity. Looking at his calm, smiling demeanor, few would guess the weight of responsibility that he carries as the spiritual Head of the Sadhu Vaswani Mission. One of his many admirable qualities is his punctuality. He carries a wrist watch and looks at it during his speeches to make sure he does not exceed the time allotted to him. In his words, "Even if I am five minutes late, I have wasted not only five minutes of my time, but five minutes of the precious time of many other people!"

He is the very epitome of compassion – compassion

towards all life. Once in Hong Kong the car in which he was traveling accidentally hit a cat which suddenly darted across the road. As soon as they reached home, though it was a late hour, Dada Jashan suggested to his hosts that they have a prayer meeting dedicated to the cat just run over. In that hushed and solemn moment, he asked for forgiveness and prayed for the cat in such a touching way that it brought tears to the eyes of those present. That night he skipped his dinner and was unusually quiet.

On another occasion, during a night walk in Pune, Dada Jashan heard the agonized howls of a dog that had been run over on the street. As it lay gasping and bleeding profusely Dada knelt down, picked it up and brought it to the side of the road. He recited a few *slokas* from the *Bhagavad Gita* and caressed the dog with his gentle hands. It was not long before the dog breathed his last. Through his words and gestures he raises those around him to a new level of awareness and sensitivity. Merely to be with him is an experience in self-unfoldment.

Repeatedly, he has stressed that his mission in life is to spread his Master's message of love and peace. As he says, "Our hearts need to be saturated with love, for love is the light which will illumine the world. More than developed brains we need enlightened hearts." That is the spirit behind the Mira Movement in Education. For as Dada Jashan points out, a brave, new world will not be built in the Senate or Parliament, but in the home and the school, for the children of today will be the builders of tomorrow. Set the child right, he says, and the world will come out right!

Dada Jashan shares the view of his Guru that the future belongs to women, for it is they who will build a new civilization, based on the ideals of simplicity, sympathy and service. It is women who will have the *shakti* to rebuild the shattered world in the strength of their intuition, purity and the spirit of silent sacrifice. It is they who will mould the children. The greatest force in the life of the community and the nation, he says, is in the home, where character is made; and it is a mother who builds a home. According to him "Home building is nation building."

Dada Jashan bears witness to his Master's teachings in deeds of daily life. Once at a *langar* (fellowship meal) at the Mission, when hundreds of devotees were being served lunch by the volunteers, Dada came by to greet everyone. Seeing all the volunteers busy with their allotted tasks, he picked up a jug of water and a bowl, and stationed himself near the door of the room where the meals were being served. The volunteers noticed this and wondered what Dada Jashan was up to. One of them asked, "Dada, is there anything we can do?"

"On the contrary," replied Dada Jashan, "since you are doing everything else, I am doing the only job left to be done. I shall pour water for the brothers and sisters to wash their hands when the *langar* is over."

No task is too low for Dada Jashan; no service too humble. His humility is not just in words and deeds; it arises so spontaneously from his heart. In his presence, people seem to absorb humility, and at least momentarily forget their inborn pride and arrogance.

Dada Jashan's universal vision, his non-sectarian approach, his avoidance of any religious bias, and his refusal to impose dogma or propagate the ritual of any particular religion has endeared him to people not only in India but around the world. As he says: "Today, in the name of religion, we have fights and feuds, sectarian strife, hatred and violence. Religion came to unite, to reconcile, to create harmony among men. Little wonder that young men and women today are turning away from religion. It is not religion which has failed us; it is we who have failed religion!"

Religion, he explains, is like our mother and all religions

are sisters. According to him true conversion is not just a change of label. Making a Hindu a Christian or vice versa is not conversion. He points out that by "conversion" Jesus meant not change of label or conformity to a creed or dogma, but a change of mind and heart. True conversion can thus lead to a change of attitude, which can ultimately result in the transformation of one's life. In the Kingdom of God, he says, we will not be judged according to our labels, but according to the life we have lived. All great religions are equally true. They are like branches of a tree, the tree of religion. This, therefore, is the essence of his message – that instead of conversion, we should rather try to be better human beings – Hindu, Christian or Muslim.

Sind is a land where prior to the tragic partition of India, Hindus and Muslims lived in peaceful co-existence. Dada J.P. Vaswani is the glorious inheritor of this rich legacy of tolerance and brotherhood. He does not merely talk about religious unity, he himself symbolises it. Thus the Mission observes not only Diwali and Dussehra, but also Christmas, Guru Nanak Jayanti, Buddha Poornima and Ramzan.

At the Tenth Hindu Conference organized by the Vishwa Hindu Parishad of America on July 7, 1984, Dada Jashan highlighted that "In spite of the ravages of time, the Hindu Faith lives on, for it has a message to give to the modern world - the message that there can be no true freedom without spirituality. The Hindu Faith is not a creed or a dogma or a ritual. It is a *darshana* and a *marga* – an insight and a way of life."

With his profound insights, Dada Jashan sums up the need of the day thus: "What humanity needs today is not merely philosophy or theology, but a message of reassurance. People need to know that they are not alone, that they have not been abandoned; but that there is One Who loves them for what they are, Who cares about them. Philosophy and theology have so much to tell us about God, but people today want to experience God. There is a difference between eating dinner and merely reading the menu."

A master psychologist, Dada Jashan knows how to handle each situation and every individual most amicably. Blest with a wonderful sense of humour, he has the knack of diffusing many a tense and stressful situation by a witty remark or a lovely joke.

Once he was asked at a question-answer session. "Which is the most important of the five senses?"

He replied: "the most important of the senses is the sixth one"

"Which is that one?"

"The sixth sense is the sense of humour."

He has always pointed out that the best kind of humour is that which makes us laugh with others and not at others. His humour is such that it never ever hurts or ridicules, it appeals to our higher selves.

During one of his several TV interviews, Dada Jashan was asked what had prompted him to choose this Path. He replied "It all happened in a most natural way – neither by design, nor by choice. When I had finished my college education, friends and relatives tried to persuade me to study for the ICS examination. It was then that my Master, Sadhu Vaswani entered my life. He awakened my slumbering soul and I realized that life is given to us not to make money or to acquire positions of power but to be poured out as a sacrifice unto the Eternal. It was my Master's doing. All glory unto him!"

The Selection of Articles in this Book

Dada Jashan is the author of more than fifty books in English and Sindhi. His books have been translated into several languages, have run into multiple editions and are always in great demand. They are an inexhaustible source of wisdom and faith for countless readers who bear witness to their power and vitality. Besides his books, he has innumerable talks to his credit, delivered at both formal and informal gatherings, in addition to his regular addresses to the *sangat* in Pune.

Dada Jashan's books and talks cover a wide range of topics. This selection of articles is taken from those writings and talks that are of particular relevance to modern life. Followers of Dada Jashan are essentially settled in urban areas, whether in India or abroad and the problems of urban life are common across the globe. More than religion or spirituality, the immediate concerns of most people, particularly the youth, is that of good health. That is why the first topic is devoted to the imperative of good health.

In an age when over-indulgence at every level seems to be the norm, good health is no longer something that can be taken for granted. Very often it is compromised because of thoughtless habits and lack of will-power. Poor health can be a great limiting factor and Dada Jashan points out some simple but profound guidelines to ensure robust health at both the physical and mental levels. In so doing he also presents some age-old concepts that spiritual seekers have adopted down the ages to keep them steady on the path to the Truth. Here are remedies that are both practical and spiritual.

Peace of mind is directly linked to good health for if an individual is constantly plagued with a sense of ill-ease and discomfort - whether physical or mental – he or she has little energy or enthusiasm for loftier preoccupations. In this section Dada Jashan analyses for us some aspects of our personalities which paralyze us, sometimes, for a lifetime. He discusses 'anger', 'stress', 'irritation' and such emotions which in themselves may not appear so significant, but which, over a period of time, rob us of that greatest of all treasures in life – peace of mind.

The first two sections thus lead us to a better understanding of ourselves. As our awareness of the working of our mind increases, we feel motivated to control ourselves and to redirect our thoughts and emotions to a nobler goal. Dada Jashan then gives us useful tips on how to rediscover the joy of living. The greatest obstacle to happiness is our inability to accept those turns of fate which are unpleasant. We forget that life is a mixture of both joy and sorrow, of pleasure and pain. Therefore, Dada points out the necessity of accepting all that comes our way with equanimity. He points out the way in which we can conquer fear because spiritual life is only for the courageous. The weak of heart are easily crushed by the smallest blows of fate. He highlights the power of a sense of humour which often enables us to lighten our load by being able to see the funny side of things. Above all, he teaches us how we can learn to laugh at ourselves.

Dada Jashan's writings lead us gradually further on the spiritual path as then he introduces us to the concept of destiny and responsibility. Everything that we do has a bearing on our future, whether immediate or distant. Similarly, everything that we have ever done – in this life or in past lives – has a bearing on our present. This understanding is vital for each one of us for it facilitates an acceptance of our situations and circumstances. It empowers us to know that we are the makers of our own destiny. It frees us of envy and jealousy when we realize that each one gets what he or she has earned. Above all, the lesson in this section is that we must take responsibility for everything we do and everything that others do to us.

This naturally leads us to the final section where we take a flight from the material into the spiritual realm. If we have carefully read and digested the earlier articles, we will have understood that life is not just lived at the physical plane which is the most obvious of all, but that there are other dimensions, more powerful, more subtle which can be grasped in silence, in prayer, in meditation. Each of us has that infinite potential to experience God. We must but listen carefully to the Master's voice. We must reflect on his words. We must surrender to him and invoke His grace so that he may clear our minds, sharpen our understanding and, most important, open the gates of our heart so that love may flow out and purify us and make us fit to walk the path.

To read these short articles of Sadhu Vaswani and Dada Jashan is to enter into contact with two great *mahatmas*. Their words carry powerful vibrations. They influence not just on our minds but also our hearts. These two volumes are, therefore, like a pilgrimage. The words and ideas that you encounter in these pages will resonate in your mind long after you have closed the book. Their fragrance will linger in your heart filling it with the peace and stillness that can only come from communion with a radiant soul

The Sadhu Vaswani Mission

The Sadhu Vaswani Mission is a humanitarian organization with his headquarters in Pune, Maharashtra. It strives to serve humanity in the fields of education and health, social work and culture and is also dedicated to the moral and spiritual upliftment of mankind. The Mission had its origin in the Sakhi Satsang founded by Sadhu Vaswani in Hyderabad, Sind, in 1931. After the Partition in 1947, when Sadhu Vaswani relocated to Pune, the mission was renamed the "Brotherhood Association." In 1966 after Sadhu Vaswani dropped his physical body the Association became the Sadhu Vaswani Mission. Today the Mission has several centres in India and across the five continents. Dada J.P. Vaswani visits these centers annually keeping in touch with his innumerable devotees.

Before he left his mortal body, Sadhu Vaswani told his devotees that he would be able to do greater things through them than he had done with his own body. That, indeed, has proved true, literally. The Mission activities have expanded considerably after the *mahasamadhi* of its founder and travel has today become an intrinsic part of Dada Jashan's life. For several months in a year he is away from his headquarters in Pune.

The pivot around which the Mission's activities revolve is the *satsang* held at least thrice daily in Pune. The devout and faithful gather for *kirtan* and *bhajan* sessions as also for recitations from the *Guru Granth Sahib* and the *Nuri Granth*. The melodious voice of Sadhu Vaswani continues to reverberate in the *satsang* that he founded, as his recorded talks still hold listeners spell-bound. On Thursday evenings and Sunday mornings, the *sangat* is privileged to hear Dada Jashan's inspiring and thrilling discourses. The last Saturday of the month is devoted to question and answer sessions with the youth. After the evening *satsang* Dada Jashan and other *satsangis* sit in quiet meditation for half an hour at Sadhu Vaswani's sacred Samadhi.

The Sadhu Vaswani Mission believes in the unity of all religions and reveres the saints and prophets of all faiths. Days sacred to them are observed with special prayer meetings and service programmes.

The Sadhu Vaswani Ashram, situated opposite the Sadhu Vaswani Mission can accommodate over 75 pilgrims who come to visit the Mission and its spiritual head. The ashram houses the Mission's *bhandara* which offers two meals to the poor and the destitute everyday. Apart from this, tea, snacks and food are also served to the homeless poor and to institutions for the underprivileged.

The Sadhu Vaswani Medical Complex, located in Koregaon

Park, Pune, is the realization of a dream of Dada J.P. Vaswani – that of a hospital where no sick person would be turned away because he was poor. Here even the lowliest of the lowly receive medical treatment. No patient here is reduced to a mere case number and each is treated with love, respect and sympathy.

The medical complex can accommodate 364 patients. It houses the Inlaks and Budhrani Hospital, the M.N. Budhrani Cancer Institute and Research Centre, the K.K. Eye Institute and the Shanti Diagnostic Clinic. The medical complex is equipped with seven operation theatres and state of the art equipment. Eminent doctors form part of its staff. Free and concessional diagnostics and treatment are offered to poor and needy patients. Donors are invited to sponsor a variety of treatments for the poor, according to their means. The Sadhu Vaswani College of Nursing ensures that well trained nurses serve the Mission and other hospitals. Other medical facilities offered by the Sadhu Vaswani Mission are those of the Mangharam Khemlani Dispensary, the Sadhu Hiranand Free Homeopathic Dispensary and the Radha Krishna Daya Dispensary.

The Mission observes February 18-24 every year as Thanksgiving Week to commemorate the successful quadruple bypass surgery performed on Dada J.P. Vaswani in the US in 1998. A special service programme has been instituted for this occasion when poor, needy patients who suffer from debilitating heart ailments are provided free diagnostic tests like the ECG, Echo and Angiography. In addition, many of them are offered free cardiac surgery.

The Sadhu Vaswani Mission has undertaken village upliftment programmes in the backward areas of Maharashtra, Saurashtra and Kutch, improving the quality of life of villagers living below the poverty line. The activities of the programme include the provision of drinking water, digging of irrigation wells, tree plantation, soil conservation, education of children, training members of households to work and become self-reliant, health camps, vocational training classes, rehabilitation of poor families, the provisions of rations and so on.

The Jiv Daya programme of the Mission undertakes the daily feeding of birds and stray animals. Sadhu Vaswani often repeated the words: "For me not to love birds and animals would be not to love the Lord." The Mission follows his precept that all life is sacred, and that birds and animals are our brothers and sisters in the one family of creation. Besides the daily feeding of birds and animals at the Sadhu Vaswani Ashram, the students of the St. Mira's Educational institutions, too, are encouraged to bring handfuls of grain, slices of bread and *chappatti* to feed birds and animals with their own hands.

One of the Mission's busiest departments, the Gita Publishing House, brings out, every year, a series of inspiring books, monthly journals and newsletters. Over 300 titles of books and booklets written by Sadhu Vaswani and Dada J.P. Vaswani in English and Sindhi have been published by the Gita Publishing House and the Mira Publications. Several of these titles have been translated into Hindi, Marathi, Gujarati and Kannada. In recent years they have also been translated into Spanish, French, German, Mandarin and Indonesian. In addition, the Mission also publishes the monthly magazines *East and West* and *Mira*. The latter is addressed to children and the youth.

The Mira Movement founded by Sadhu Vaswani in 1933 today has six educational institutions in Pune, in which over 6000 students study, from the pre-primary right up to the post-graduate level. The aim of the Mira Movement in Education is not just to make students pass examinations and acquire degrees but to impart a character building, man-making education with its emphasis on the integration of head, hand and heart.

While still in Sind, the Movement was to have developed

a Mira University when the Partition put an end to this noble effort. However, a St. Mira's College was established in Pune in 1962. Professor K.N. Vaswani, one of the editors of the *Collected Works of Mahatma Gandhi* was appointed as the first Principal of the college. After him, Dada Jashan was asked to step into his shoes as no suitable candidate could be found. Dadaji worked as the Honorary Principal of St. Mira's College for sixteen long years and during this period the college grew from a small plant into a huge, sheltering tree. Starting with only sixty-two young women, the college today has over three thousand students.

Besides being the Principal, Dada J. P. Vaswani also taught in the college. His lectures on Civilization Science were immensely popular for he blended his lessons with anecdotes, general knowledge and jokes. His lecture period always started with a short prayer. Punctuality marked his classes and students were expected to respect time as he always did.

No student is ever turned away from any Mira Institution for lack of money. Dada's devotees have proved to be benevolent donors, offering scholarships and other forms of financial aid to such students. Books, notebooks, food, clothes and even transport costs are provided to them. All help is extended to them discreetly, without fanfare. Today the Sadhu Vaswani Mission also runs other educational institutions such as the Sadhu Vaswani International School for girls in Delhi and the Sadhu Vaswani International School in Hyderabad and in Navi Mumbai. The latter two are co-educational institutions.

Although the Sadhu Vaswani Mission functions for humanity in general, its main focus and concern is the Sindhi community. It feels responsible for the community that was scattered across India and the world after 1947 and it has taken the initiative of propagating the Sindhi language, in particular. Sindhis have no land that they can call their own. Consequently, Sindhi is a language without any political value.

As a result, it is dying out. With the disappearance of the Sindhi language, Sindhi identity is threatened. This is particularly so in the case of Sindhis because, being extremely adjusting, they have readily adopted the language, the dress and the ways of the host societies where they have settled. Hence, it is often difficult to distinguish them from the people among whom they live. Dada Jashan believes that there is only one thing that can bring all the Sindhis together, and that is their language. The Sindhi language, even a smattering of it, instantly establishes a bond between members of the community. Therefore, one of the important thrusts of the Sadhu Vaswani Mission has been to keep the language alive. Special short crash courses are organized at the Headquarters in Pune, particularly during the vacations and these are availed of by Sindhis visiting Pune from around the world. These courses have steadily gained popularity with the younger generation. An increasing number of students have learnt to read and write Sindhi in the original Arabic script, or even in Devnagari, as an easier modern alternative. To many earnest Sindhi-lovers, these classes have opened the door to the vast literary treasures which exist in the Sindhi language.

Concern for propagating the Sindhi language is also the reason why most of the work of the mission is done in this medium. The mission would, undoubtedly, draw a bigger audience if it used English or Hindi but then the Sindhi language would die out. Sadhu Vaswani believed, as does Dada J.P. Vaswani, that the rich treasure of Sindhi literature has a message to give to the world. Sadhu Vaswani's own contribution to the Sindhi language has been invaluable. His many inspired writings and his collection of poems entitled the *Nuri Granth* are outstanding works judged by any literary standard. The *Nuri Granth* is a collection of over 4000 songs and 2000 *slokas*, perhaps the longest and greatest work of a single poet-saint in any language. Its poetic merit is of a high order. Its emotional appeal is profound and its spiritual intensity is powerful.

Dada J.P. Vaswani, and the Sadhu Vaswani Mission, renewed their connection with Sind in 2005 when Dada Jashan returned to the land of his birth after 57 long years. The visit was at the invitation of the D.J. Sindh Government College, Karachi, and the Sind Graduates' Association. Dada Jashan took with him the message of friendship and cooperation between the people of India and Pakistan. He called for a breaking down of the barriers in the hearts of people, invoking the spirit of the Sind of by-gone days, a Sind where generosity, tolerance and hospitality were legendary.

The Sadhu Vaswani Mission's work is possible because of large-scale donations from Sindhis. In fact, Sindhis constitute 99% of the donors but represent only about 15% of the beneficiaries of the Mission's charity work. The hospital and programmes such as charitable feeding are enjoyed by all communities.

For a number of years after the *mahasamadhi* of Sadhu Vaswani, Dada Jashan made only short trips out of Pune. It was only in 1982 that he made his first overseas *yatra*. This was to address a conference organized by the World Hindu Conference in Colombo. Hearing of this visit to Colombo, several invitations from devotees in the East and West poured in. So Dada Jashan agreed to visit a few Far-Eastern countries in addition to Sri Lanka. Wherever he goes, whichever city, town or country he visits, he repeatedly urges his Sindhi brothers and sisters not to forget their sacred mother tongue.

On numerous occasions, Dada Jashan has addressed several world forums such as the United Nations, the British House of Commons, the World Convention of Religious and Spiritual Leaders, or International Conferences on World Peace, to name just a few. He has always responded to invitations from other spiritual institutions like the Chinmaya Mission,

the Ramakrishna Math or the Hope Foundation and other professional organizations like the CII (Chamber of Indian Industry) or the State Chambers of Commerce or Doctors' Associations, the Rotary International and so on. To him they are all working towards the one goal. He has also been invited to speak at several Universities around the world.

Sadhana camps are a unique feature of Dada Jashan's visits and they have gained great popularity in India as well as abroad. The three-day camp is an uplifting experience which includes guided meditations, yoga, *akhand kirtan*, service activities, games, cultural programmes, question-answer sessions, campfire and discourses by Dada.

Since 1986, the Mission celebrates Sadhu Vaswani's birthday as the International Meatless Day. Dada Jashan personally led the initial campaign which appealed to people to abstain from all food of violence on this one day, sacred to the memory of his Beloved Master. There is no more fitting a tribute that could be paid to the prophet of compassion, who regarded all creation as one family, and who looked upon birds and animals as man's younger brothers and sisters.

Over the years the Meatless Day Campaign has gathered tremendous momentum. Four state governments in India (Maharashtra, Gujarat, Karnataka and Andhra Pradesh) have issued instructions for the closure of slaughter-houses as well as butchers' shops on 25th November, every year, in their respective states. Thousands of students from city schools and colleges march through the streets propagating the idea of Meatless Day and reverence for all life, as the first step to World Peace. Meatless Newsletters are also issued between August and November every year to propagate vegetarianism and the Meatless Day. Even countries as distant as Brazil have responded enthusiastically to this campaign of compassion. Devotees in America have put the Meatless Day Campaign on the Net. Every year millions of pledges are received from people who vow to go meatless on this day. Since 1996 this day has been declared as Animal Rights Day. As always, Dada Jashan is the motivating force behind the campaign, the ultimate goal of which is to have November 25 declared as World Animal Rights Day.

A second important date for Mission members is August, 2, the birthday of Dada Jashan. In fact, the entire first week of August is a period of great celebration for members of the Mira institutions, devotees and well-wishers alike. Dada Jashan requests people not to offer him worldly gifts. Instead, he urges the schools and college to perform special social service activities during the week to show their love and regard for him.

Thousands of devotees around the world, look upon Dada Jashan as their Guru and mentor. When they are lonely or feel isolated, they seek his companionship. They turn to him for light and wisdom. To many, he represents a living God on earth. But Dada, with his characteristic humility, denies that he is a guru at all. "I am a guru of none; I am a disciple of all," he says, gently brushing aside people's tendency to worship him.

Dada Jashan has a close group of disciples, but the one who has devoted her entire life to his service is Krishna Kumari. This young woman came into Sadhu Vaswani's life when she was just three years old. Her aunt, Sati Thadani, who was one of the greatest devotees of Sadhu Vaswani, once brought her little niece to visit the great Master. After this first meeting the little girl refused to go home. She insisted upon remaining with Sadhu Vaswani and, with his permission, became a permanent part of the household. After the *mahasamadhi* of Sadhu Vaswani, Krishna remained a part of the household and became the completely surrendered disciple of Dada Jashan. A brilliant student who completed her M.Com with distinction, Krishna refused to pursue a career, preferring to remain in the service of her Master. She manages everything from the material and mundane to the spiritual and looks into every detail of the activities of her Master and his Mission.

....

Healthy Mind, Healthy Body

We feel exhausted, again and again,
because we are not in contact with the
source of strength and inspiration which
is within us. Our interior life is starved.
Strength is needed. Therefore, we must
cultivate the soul!

J. P. Vaswani

1
THE WAY TO GOOD HEALTH

Man is a combination of the body, mind and soul. If he is to live a happy, healthy and harmonious life, all these three aspects of his being must co-operate with each other. They must not pull in different directions. They must not work against each other.

In the *Bhagavad Gita*, Lord Krishna reminds Arjuna, his devoted disciple, that he is not the body. The body, Krishna explains, is but a garment worn by you. You are something else, you are the wearer of the garment. Man, as our ancient scriptures have taught us, is essentially a soul, who has worn a body, and brought with himself the equipment of the mind, to be able to do his work on this earth. This, in essence, is the Eastern concept of being.

The Western view, however, is different. In the West they believe that man is a body, with a mind and soul in it. The emphasis here is on the body, while the Eastern view emphasizes the soul. I only come to remind you that each one of you is essentially a soul. Each one of you is that *atman*, the Spirit that never dies.

Heath, wholeness, holiness – did you know that these words have a common root? There is a prayer which I offer to God again and again. I would like to share it with you. It is a short prayer and it is non-credal. Any man belonging to any faith can offer it to God:

God, grant me health,
Grant me wholeness,
Grant me holiness!

As you offer this prayer again and again, a day will come when it will be touched with deep feeling, deep emotion arising out of the very depths of your heart. Then you will find that your mind is filled with peace that passeth, surpasseth understanding and your body becomes vibrant and vital!

Alas, for many people, life is not the joyous harmonious experience that it ought to be. They go through life only half alive – they do not live, they merely exist. I am not talking about the poor, the deprived or the malnourished. I am talking about the "better class" of people, who are in no better state of health, for riches cannot buy good health. As the saying goes, money can buy the most comfortable mattress, but it cannot buy you a night's peaceful sleep. Money can buy you the most expensive meal in a 5-star hotel, but it cannot buy you a healthy appetite. Money can buy you the best medical care, but it cannot buy you good health.

That is why our ancestors insisted: when wealth is lost, very little is lost; but when health is lost, something valuable is lost. Indeed, the wanton waste and abuse of our health is a far more serious matter than the simple waste of money. Good health is the greatest of all gifts, the choicest of all blessings, for without it, we cannot enjoy any of our other faculties and blessings.

Good health is the basis of all that we value and cherish in human life – success, achievement, financial prosperity, emotional security, and above all, spiritual unfoldment and inner peace.

It has been well established through research and case-studies that all major illnesses of the body are linked to negative emotions. In other words, a negatively inclined mind causes physical ailments in the body. Negative emotions create chaos and agitation in the mind, which affect the vital functions of the body. For example, anger and tension release harmful toxins into the bloodstream. On the other hand, goodness and sympathy promote the healthy flow of pure blood to the brain, stimulating the brain cells.

Deep breathing, meditation and virtuous living help you overcome infirmities. They infuse vitality and energy into the body. Silence and prayer put an end to nervous tension. Tranquility clears the complexion and lends lustre to your face. Happiness regulates your blood circulation. Sympathy strengthens the nerves, and generosity keeps your heart healthy and fit!

Many of us have come to accept ill-health as a matter of course. Pain, sickness, ulcers, aches, abnormal growths, weariness – all these have become as inevitable as inflation, taxation and bad weather. There is no need to accept ill-health with such a sense of stoicism and helplessness. We can and must take matters into our own hands!

It is a clinically proven fact that your body reacts to your attitude. I know bankers and financiers who have suffered a heart attack when their investments proved to be bad. Equally, I have known chronically ill patients revive miraculously when a marriage is announced or a baby is born in the family. Bad news can make you ill – and good news can make you well. Negative emotions create an imbalance in your body, leading to ill health; positive emotions restore the balance, bringing good health. Your body reacts to your attitude and changes your life. You can change your attitude and choose good health!

Sickness is not a punishment. It is the effect of a cause for which you are responsible. Choosing tension instead of tranquility, choosing stress instead of serenity, choosing indulgence instead of moderation, choosing bad instead of good, we make ourselves ill!

It is only in recent years that we have come to understand the full extent of what we now call Emotionally Induced Illness – EII. Some doctors think EII is responsible for as much as 95% of all sickness..

Anger, fear, envy, jealousy, worry…in fact the seven deadly sins of medieval Christian theology – pride, covetousness, lust, anger, gluttony, envy and sloth – any of these can make you ill; more than one can keep you ill for a long time; and a group of them can actually kill you. A medical researcher, I read, describes the seven deadly sins as sins against common sense!

We all recognize that other people make themselves ill. "She is killing herself with overwork,", we say. "He is driving himself to an early grave with all that drinking!" or "He eats so much that he is going to burst one of these days!" but, alas, we cannot apply it to ourselves. We fail to see how we are making ourselves ill! If illness were indeed a punishment, then we are punishing ourselves!

Even orthopedic complaints are emotionally induced. Bad posture, lack of exercise, prolonged standing or sitting can cause problems like backache, slipped disc and muscular spasm. Of course there are such things as hereditary diseases, birth defects or congenital disabilities and ailments caused by accidents. These are outside our control, but the vast majority of human illnesses are emotionally induced. Therefore, I say to you again: Good health is a gift you can give yourself.

Longevity is not the primary goal of human life. We are told that life expectancy has increased in our times and this is attributed to better health care and the advances made in medicine and allied sciences. But a longer life is not what all of us seek. A life of pain and disease and affliction can only be a miserable burden, when it is prolonged. Thus we have the cases of incurable diseases, and people who are clinically dead being put on life-support systems in the ICUs of hospitals. This is hardly the kind of treatment or 'life' that we aspire to!

Take the case of a man who is not really ill. He may not suffer from any disease, but he may feel dull, lethargic and listless. He may be unhappy and beset by negative emotions. Such a man is not really healthy.

Every year people spend millions of rupees on drugs, pills, painkillers and antibiotics. I am not including the soaring costs of hospitalization or surgery. I am merely talking about out-patient prescriptions and medication. In fact, most people would agree that excessive use of barbiturates, tranquilizers and analgesics is one of the major social problems of today.

We could do away with all these drugs – and with dangerous addictions like tobacco and alcohol – if we change our attitude! So you know what this means? It means that you can choose good health as your birthright! And you can do that by keeping the five following points in mind:

- Induce happiness into your life! Act happy and cheerful.
- Radiate an atmosphere of calm and serenity around you.
- Do not envy anybody.
- Avoid anticipating anything bad.
- Practice relaxation techniques consciously.

All systems of medicine and surgery are based on the fact that the body is a self-healing mechanism. Drugs are prescribed only to ease symptoms. Surgery is performed to bring cut parts of the body together, after removing infected parts. In either case the doctor knows that if the patient is made to rest in comfort, the healing process of the body will take care of the rest. If you find this difficult to believe, just consider how the body's defenses rush to the site of the wound when you cut yourself. In a trice, the bleeding stops; in a while, the healing starts; in a few days the wound is closed and the skin is new!

I remember the words of the great comedian, Charlie Chaplin. He said: "When I fall sick, I go to the doctor. After all, the doctor has to live! The doctor writes out a prescription for me and I take it to the chemist – for the chemist too must live! The chemist gives me medicines – but I don't take them, for I too must live!"

You are your own healer. The power of healing is within you. And the time has come when doctors too have realized that they must work, not on the disease and its symptoms, but on this principle of healing that is within each one of us. True health and well-being encompass man's physical, mental, intellectual and spiritual state. When there is harmony and integrity between all these states, a man is in good health. This is the concept of holistic health that we need now.

2
SELF-DISCIPLINE – BRAHMACHARYA

A sage was sitting on the top of a mountain, silent, thoughtful, engrossed in deep meditation. His eyes were bright, his face was radiant. He seemed to glow with good health. Placed before him was a jug of water.

A villager who saw the sage was so impressed by him, that he begged the wise man, "O sir, tell me the secret of your wisdom and the sparkle in your eyes!"

The sage replied, "I fast, I meditate, I sip this water when I am thirsty – and that is all I do."

"The secret must be in the water!" exclaimed the villager. "O wise man! Give me some of that water – and name your price!"

Reluctantly, the sage agreed to give the man a pitcher of water in return for a gold coin.

The villager eagerly gulped down the water and waited for a miracle. Obviously, no miracle was forthcoming. Reviewing his transaction gloomily, he concluded, "I was a fool to pay you for this water! I should have gone to the stream and got it for nothing!"

"Ah!" exclaimed the sage. "So you are becoming wiser already!"

The secret of the sage's wisdom was not in the water or indeed in the meditation or fasting, though people have always believed that these can lead to wisdom and emotional well-being. It is of course true, but the underlying principle of fasting and meditation is self-discipline. Self-discipline is perhaps the most under-rated and least recognized virtue these days. I always say that self-discipline is the exercise of our spiritual muscles!

Any weight-lifter will tell you that he started off with light weights and then progressed to heavier tasks. So it is with self-discipline. We must begin with easy conquests, simple sacrifices and little acts of self-denial. This will pave the way for our spiritual progress on the path of *brahmacharya* – walking with God.

Unfortunately many people today are reluctant to deny themselves the least pleasure or gratification. The child must have its chocolate or ice-cream, the teenager must have his pizza and his loud music; the young adult must have his cigarette and his fast bike, and the grown-ups (who ought to know better) must have their drinks, their parties and their superficial social life. No one is prepared to give up anything. Instant gratification is the order of the day!

Self-discipline requires effort, but its rewards are very many! Addiction to drugs, alcoholism and sexual indulgence can all be conquered through the practice of self-discipline. We may even begin to dream of a society in which there is no crime, no prostitution, no drink or disorderly conduct! In other words, we may actually begin to visualize man evolving into a superior being! Difficult – but not impossible!

Gluttony, lust and self-indulgence are among the deadliest sins of mankind. They represent the coils of the biblical serpent which is said to have tempted Eve to commit the offence which lost paradise for mankind, according to Christian belief.

Throughout ancient folklore and myth, the serpent has always symbolized lust. The serpent must be conquered – not by sword or spear – but through spiritual discipline and self-denial. This can truly free us from the deadly coils of the serpent.

Alas, we live in a world where old-fashioned virtues, like self-denial, self-discipline and self-restraint are no longer valued. Ours is the age of materialism and mass consumption. Everywhere hoardings proclaim – Buy now – pay later! Enjoy yourself – we'll take care of the rest! Borrow more money – no questions asked! Gratify your appetite here and now! They might as well tell us – indulge yourself now, suffer later!

"Many are the keys to good health", Mahatma Gandhi tells us. "No doubt they are all essential; but the one thing needful, above all others, is *brahmacharya*."

Brahmacharya is freedom from lust and carnality. In other words, it is freedom from the coils of the serpent. Today, for the sake of momentary pleasure we sacrifice what is most valuable – spiritual energy. How wisely has Shakespeare written:

The expense of spirit in a waste of shame
Is lust in action....

Gandhiji observed the sad spectacle of the world around him, and saw that men and women, old and young, without exception, were entangled in the coils of sensuality and lust. It seemed to him that people had actually turned mad under this pernicious influence. And all for what? Do we not pay a heavy price for momentary indulgence?

Excessive indulgence in sensuality is the root-cause of several mental and physical ailments. We have seen that good health is impossible without pure air, pure water, pure and wholesome food, as well as pure thoughts. In fact, I would go so far as to say that we can never be perfectly healthy unless we lead a clean life.

All the major religions of the world talk about the necessity of self-discipline, especially the control of the lower passions. However, the Hindu scriptures have attached a profound significance to the concept of *brahmacharya*. As we saw earlier, Sadhu Vaswani defined *brahmacharya* in a beautiful way – walking with God. Literally, the term also means living and moving with Brahman – the Absolute, Divine Self. In its highest form, it implies consciousness of the concept – *Aham Brahmasmi* – I am Brahman. Thus it relates to the effort to realize our divine potential.

In a more limited sense, *brahmacharya* implies the practice of celibacy and restraint of sex indulgences. Thus in ancient India, young disciples and students learning at the feet of a guru in an ashram were enjoined not to indulge in sensual pleasures and to observe strict celibacy, until they were old enough and mature enough to enter the next stage of life – the *grihastha ashrama* or married life.

Although celibacy and restraint are undoubtedly important aspect of *brahmacharya*, in a broader sense it implies conquest over passions and the sublimation of the merely biological instinct leading to a profound perception of the Self in relation to the Universe.

Further, *brahmacharya* in this broader sense, can be understood and practiced by people of all ages, married and unmarried. When a married couple begins to realize that physical relationship is not an end in itself, they will find that they can relate to each other at a more profound and meaningful level. When we reach this state, we become capable of inner creativity and fulfillment. We grow in spiritual evolution and develop an intuitive intellect. The illusion of pleasure and deluding happiness of the world are left behind as we enter a stage of creative consciousness that is the Spirit. Your thoughts will be clean, your mind more sensitive, and your soul in tune with the deep harmony of the Universe.

This is what yoga terms as *ojas shakti* – i. e. sublimated sexual energy. What are the attributes of *ojas shakti?* A mind that vibrates spiritual strength and a radiance which surrounds you with an effulgent brilliance!

All happily married couples know that a meaningful relationship is one in which the partners learn to minimize selfish demands upon each other and acquire the virtues of patience, understanding, tolerance and self-sacrifice. Thus they promote their own spiritual evolution, and rise above the kind of superficial love that is only an entanglement.

The ideal of *brahmacharya* does not regard sex a shame and sin – but considers it as a creative force which is not to be squandered or abused. For when it is misused, sexual energy generates several negative qualities like pride, egoism, jealousy, anger and greed in the human psyche.

Gandhiji was asked, "If all men would turn *brahmacharis,* would not humanity be extinct?"

His answer was simple: "Do not look for excuses! *Brahmacharis* are not to be had for the asking – for they are as rare and precious as diamonds. We only reveal our weakness and cowardice, when we look for such pretexts. Instead we should keep this idea constantly before us, and try to achieve it to the utmost of our capacity."

Those who have practiced *brahmacharya* even for a short period can vouch for the fact that body, mind and spirit gain in strength and power. Their energy and enthusiasm is greater, and they attain to a higher form of joy which transcends the mind's quest for lower and lesser pleasures.

In its broadest sense, *brahmacharya* denotes purity of character, purity of thought, word and deed. It denotes mastery over the mind and senses, especially over the sexual force. For when the latter is brought under control, all other aspects of our life are automatically brought under control. Such a state of self-discipline is conducive to our health, happiness and spiritual progress. Indeed, *brahmacharya* is a virtue that will help us to lead an active and healthy life for a long period of time.

I am aware that people will find it strange that I talk about *brahmacharya*, which is associated especially with the practice of celibacy, in an age when sexual promiscuity has become rampant. I would only like to remind you that it was "free sex" of this sort that destroyed the ancient civilizations of Babylon, Greece and Rome.

Brahmacharya, as I have said, goes beyond the concept of celibacy and it includes purification and awakening of consciousness. Such a state of consciousness surely cannot tolerate moral aberrations like the legalization of abortion and immoral relationships outside marriage.

What we need under the circumstances is a change of mind, a change of attitude, a transformation of the heart. Suppression or repression will harm us – while transformation of the mind will be a positive effort. And we would also do well to remember that an idle mind is the devil's workshop. An active, useful life with meditation and *naam-japa* in leisure hours will help us lead a well-balanced life.

The mind must be controlled and disciplined to promote mental well-being. Purity of mind is one of the greatest blessings a man or woman can achieve. Regularity, punctuality, clean habits, *satvic* food and yoga exercises are all beneficial in the practice of *brahmacharya*.

Dhanvantri was a great physician of antiquity. In several Hindu temples in south India, he is worshipped as a Divine Healer – an aspect of Lord Vishnu Himself. He was regarded as the physician of the three worlds, and as the founder of the system of Ayurveda. One of his students in ayurveda came to him and sought his blessings.

"I will begin my work of healing people now," he said to the master in reverence. "Bless me, and give me a rule of health which I can propagate among my patients so that they may lead a health life."

Dhanvantari said to him, "Remember this, that *veerya*, the seminal fluid, the seminal energy, the seminal force is an aspect of God Himself. Conserve it, and you will live a long and healthy life. Waste it – and you will be burdened with an unhealthy life."

I do not need to dilate more on this. You know the truth of this: purity is life; sensuality is death. This is the law of life; this is the law of good health.

3
THE VEGETARIAN DIET

In practical terms food can be of two categories: food of violence – *himsa* –that includes fish, flesh and fowl; and food of *ahimsa* or non-violence – in other words, a vegetarian diet.

During the last fifty years or more, medical experts and nutritionists have largely inclined to the opinion that a vegetarian diet is the best option for good health. Anatomical and physiological studies point to the fact that civilized, evolved man is meant to be a vegetarian. His entire digestive system, including his teeth, his stomach and his intestines are so structured as to prove that even nature meant him to be a vegetarian.

There are some people who claim that milk is an animal product and therefore should not be included in a strictly vegetarian diet. But the fact remains, that we do not kill a cow to obtain its milk.

Mahatma Gandhi who was an ardent advocate of a vegan diet – one which does not include any animal product whatsoever – excluded milk totally from his diet for about six years or so. Then in 1917, he fell ill, and in his own words "was reduced to a skeleton." The doctors warned him that he would not be able to build up enough strength to leave his bed, if milk and milk products were not included in his diet. However, Gandhiji had made a vow that he would not take milk. A doctor then suggested to him that when he had made the vow, he could only have had in mind the milk of the cow and the buffalo, so the vow should not prevent him from taking goat's milk! That was how Gandhiji began to take goat's milk. At that time, he himself admitted, it seemed to bring him new life! He picked up rapidly and was soon able to leave his sickbed. On account of this and several similar experiences, he writes, "I have been forced to admit the necessity of adding milk to the strict vegetarian diet."

The arguments in favour of a vegetarian diet fall under four categories:

1. Physiological: Flesh diet is held to be responsible for serious diseases such as cancer.

2. Moral and ethical: There is much to be said against the wanton cruelty inflicted upon dumb and defenseless animals.

3. Economic: It has been proved that equal or better nutrition can be obtained from vegetable food more efficiently and economically than from flesh foods.

4. Aesthetic: No one is every put off by the sight of a salad or other vegetarian preparations!

However, we are now looking at a vegetarian diet in relation to the maintenance of good health in human beings. Millions of individuals all over the world subsist entirely on a vegetarian diet; and they have remained in good health and led very productive lives. Nutritionally, the only possible justification for a flesh diet is the necessity for protein. But it has been amply demonstrated that sufficient protein can be obtained from non-animal sources such as *dals*, beans, lentils, nuts, and so on.

If there is one thing that people have come to fear as much as a nuclear explosion, it is that dreaded substance called cholesterol. An increased level of cholesterol in the blood is responsible for coronary heart disease and also gall-stones. It is now a well-known fact that animal fats raise the cholesterol level in the blood. Further, the saturated fatty acids in animal fat aggravate coronary heart disease.

Cholesterol is actually a steroid present in all animal cells. It occurs in almost all food of animal origin, such as meat, fish, milk, cream, cheese, eggs and butter. Cholesterol is present in the *fat* portion of these foods. Most foods of plant origin such as fruits, vegetables and cereals do not contain cholesterol. Research has proved that animal fats raise the cholesterol level of the blood, while certain vegetables actually lower it.

Another factor we must consider in evaluating the health aspects of a non-vegetarian diet is the amount of toxic wastes present in the flesh of a dead animal. They are very high. Thus, when we eat the flesh of animals, we are not only consuming the so-called nutritive portions, but also these poisonous waste-products. It is not possible for the body to eliminate these poisons immediately and effectively.

A number of people are under the impression that they and their children cannot be strong unless they eat food of violence. It is only meat and chicken and eggs which can give strength to the body, they say. Without this type of food, will not the body become weak, and a prey to many diseases?

As an answer to this query, we can cite the example of the elephant, which is one of the biggest and strongest animals in the world. As we all know, it is a pure vegetarian! Yet another vegetarian animal is the camel, which carries heavy loads across endless, burning desert sands!

"What of the lion?" someone may ask. The elephant cannot match its strength against the power and fury of a lion. True, but the lion has destructive strength, while the elephant has productive strength that can be used in the service of humanity. The elephant carries huge logs of wood across the teak forests of Burma even today. Can we make a lion do something like this? Perhaps yes – but only in a circus; or outside, at the risk of our life!

Another erroneous belief is that one cannot get sufficient protein from a vegetarian diet. Meat, it is said, is the only source of protein that can be of use to us. Our protein need varies from individual to individual. It depends upon a person's weight, sex and the type of work he does. If you take more protein than is required by your body, it may lead to degenerative diseases like osteoporosis and obesity. The average minimum protein requirement of a man or woman is estimated to be around 45 gms. a day. This is easily available in milk (preferably skimmed, so as to remove excess fat), curds, cheese, lentils, soya, beans, peanuts and sunflower seeds.

In quality too, the protein in vegetarian food is superior to that obtained from flesh food. Dr. Christopher Gian Cuisio, a nutritionist of repute, tells us that, "vegetables are primary sources nourished by the sun and soil, while meat is a secondary source nourished and sustained by vegetables." Most of the animals killed for food, live on a vegetarian diet. Why then, should we not go to the source of all nutrition – vegetarian food?

4

THE BENEFITS OF FASTING

What is fasting? Fasting means abstaining from all food and leaving the stomach empty for a few hours or a few days. This is *not* to be confused with starving, for fasting is undertaken intentionally with the aim of cleansing or detoxifying the system. By abstaining from all food and restricting our system to the intake of water or liquids alone, we enable our system to clean itself.

During a fast all the toxic wastes accumulated in the body are thrown out in the form of phlegm, faeces or gas. The reserves – in some cases, the excess – of carbohydrates, fats and vitamins that have been built up in our system, are used up efficiently and effectively. The body becomes light, agile and alert. No harmful side effects are produced.

Is there an optimum period of fasting? Obviously this will vary from person to person. Many people undertake to fast once a week, for a day. Others undertake fasts for three days, a week or even ten days. Medical experts agree that such short fasts will produce all the beneficial effects of longer fasts, which are undertaken only by a few people with a definite moral or spiritual purpose. As we saw earlier, the body builds up a reserve out of the excess carbohydrates and fats that we consume. It is only the excess of this reserve that is used up when we fast. Most doctors feel that this reserve is sufficient to meet the requirements of an otherwise healthy person for 40 days. Most of us can easily fast for up to three days, experiencing only minor discomforts. As for people who suffer from chronic conditions, they can undertake short fasts with the intake of certain foods, under the guidance of experts.

One thing to be noted about fasting is that after 48 hours, in most cases, all sensations of hunger will disappear. People who undertake longer fasts on a regular basis tell us that they themselves come to know when the fast is to be broken, by the re-appearance of hunger, which indicates that the system is cleansed and ready to return to its routine. This is accompanied by other indications. The coated tongue becomes clear; the whites of the eyes become clear; the pulse and the heart rate return to normal; and the senses become sharp and alert.

When a small child is unwell, he or she refuses all food. The tendency of the mother is to coax the child to eat a little; at times, she even feeds the child forcefully for she imagines that missing a meal is akin to a severe deprivation. Ancient wisdom, however, tells us that fasting is the supreme medicine. Even sick animals will refuse to touch food, for fasting is nature's treatment to respond to most disorders that afflict us.

"Take away food from a sick man", says an eminent doctor, "and you have begun not to starve the sick man, but the disease." The best treatment for most ailments is abstinence from eating. It is only in the case of debilitating diseases such as TB that fasting is not recommended.

People today are so addicted to eating that they even snack between two main meals. Even when they work, they take a coffee break or tea break. When they go to the movies, they take popcorn or chocolate or ice-cream with them. When they have nothing to do, they eat just to pass the time. When they watch TV they like to munch on something. Thus, constant eating has become part of our social behaviour. Some people even get up from sleep for a midnight snack! How can the human digestive system function efficiently when it is constantly misused in this way? It is little wonder that digestive disorders are common among the affluent nowadays.

Our ancestors knew the remedy for it – habitual fasting on certain days of the week or month. Thus people in India still observe a fast on holy days such as *ekadashi, chaturthi* or on certain days of the week like Mondays or Saturdays.

Alas, many of us lead sedentary lives, nor do we get sufficient exercise to utilize the large quantities of food that we regularly consume. All the surplus intake clogs the system with toxins and impurities. The digestive tract is overburdened. Both digestion and elimination are slowed down and body functions become distorted. This vicious cycle – over eating and retention of waste – is the root cause of several chronic disorders.

Fasting is an excellent process of self-discipline. It is one of the safest and quickest ways to rid the body of toxins. Fasting is also one of the best ways to clear the brain, enabling it to operate at peak efficiency. The Red Indians of America believed that fasting gave rise to wisdom.

Most religions of the world recommend fasting to the devout. Christians fast during Lent. Jews fast on the even of all their feasts. Muslims fast during Ramzan. Hindus fast on *ekadashi* and *chaturthi* days.

Mahatma Gandhi fasted several times during his life – often up to twenty days or more. He fasted not only for health, but also for moral and political considerations. Even after India's independence, he fasted to reconcile Hindus and Muslims in Calcutta. A medical friend once requested him to put down in writing, the effects of fasting as observed in his own experience. Gandhiji gladly complied with his request, for he had seen that many people had done themselves harm by the wrong approach to fasting. He saw himself as an "inveterate diet reformer" and a great believer in fasting, even though most of his fasts had been undertaken for moral or political purposes. Here are some of the 'rules' that he was able to deduce from his own experience, which he recommends to people who wish to undertake fasts for a longer duration than 24 hours:

1) Conserve your energy, both physical and mental, from the beginning. Do not attempt any strenuous physical activity.

2) Try not to think of food when you are fasting.

3) Drink as much water as you can – with or without a little salt, soda or fresh lime. The water should preferably be boiled, strained and cooled.

4) Have a warm sponge bath daily, during the period of the fast.

5) Sunlight and fresh air are essential to the system. Expose yourself to both in the morning.

6) If you are fasting for a long period, make sure that you eliminate the waste from your system regularly.

7) No matter from what motive you are fasting – during this precious time, think of your Maker, and of your relation to His creation.

Gandhiji adds that the physical and moral effects of fasting are being recognized more and more every day. Several diseases can be treated more effectively by judicious fasting, rather than by drugs, for drugs cause more mischief than we are aware of. However, not many cases of harm done by fasting can be cited. In fact, it is the universal experience of people who have fasted, that they feel an increased level of vitality. This is because real rest for the mind and body is possible only during fasting. A day off from work does not give us real rest – for our overtaxed and overworked digestive apparatus hardly ever gets the rest it deserves!

The moral effects of fasting are considerable but they are not so easy to demonstrate. Gandhiji wisely warns us against the damages of self-deception in this context, and quotes the warning given by Prophet Muhammad to his followers who imitated his fasts: "My Maker sends me food enough when I fast, not so to you", he told them. To this, Gandhiji adds, "Of what use is a spiritual fast when the spirit hankers after food?"

We would do well to keep in mind that fasting is not a miracle cure: its effectiveness is dependant on giving our vital organs a much needed rest. This also allows the inherent healing influences of the body to accomplish their work without interference.

When the fast is to be terminated, it is important to break it in the right manner. Depending on the length of the fast, the person should take fresh fruit juice or vegetable juice to begin with; this can be followed by soft fruits a little later; in fact, it is recommended that an all-fruit diet for two or three days should follow the fast. Later, salads and nuts can be added and a regular diet resumed on the fifth day. Above all, it is important that we do not lose all the benefits we have gained from the fast by returning to the wrong eating and living habits.

5

THE POWER OF THOUGHT

Take care of your thoughts! For thoughts have power over the body; they have an almost instantaneous effect on the glands of the body. That is why we often say that when we think of a delicious dessert or a favourite dish, we begin to salivate – the salivary glands, in this case, are activated by mere thought.

I repeat, thoughts affect your body, therefore be conscious of your thoughts. Our minds today are full of wrong thoughts, negative thoughts. We allow our minds to be filled with thoughts of illness, pain, disease, thoughts of passion, pride, lust, greed, hatred, and resentment, thoughts of ill-will, envy and jealousy. With such thoughts darkening our hearts and minds, how can we expect to be healthy and happy?

A healthy mind is a healthy body: this has become a clichéd expression. But, like so many clichés it reminds us of a neglected truth: one cannot enjoy physical well-being without mental well-being. Nutritious food, fresh air, regular exercise, good habits, clean environment, and a sober lifestyle are all essential to our well-being; but the right attitude, the right state of mind and right thinking are indispensable. For man is not just the body: he is a composite of body, mind, intellect and spirit.

Great thinkers and philosophers down the ages have different views on several issues but they have agreed unanimously on one point – we become what we think.

It was Emerson who said, "A man is what he thinks about all day long." The Bible tells us the same thing: "As man thinks in his heart, so is he." Marcus Aurelius, the great Roman thinker, puts it this way: "A man's life is what his thoughts make of it."

I have met some people who make their ailments and disabilities into a veritable calling card. They flaunt their diseases almost like badges of honour. The polite greeting, "How are you?" is enough to make them launch into a litany of their numerous bodily afflictions. Such an attitude acts as a resistance to the healing energy that is available to us all. When we wallow in our misery and pain, we are only clinging to them. Such people are constantly focusing on disharmony and disease.

In an inspiring book called *The Power of Intention*, Dr. Wayne W. Dyer, best selling author, tells us that if we wish to be healthy, we must stop seeing ourselves as the physical body, and immerse ourselves in the idea of absolute well-being. "Breathe only wellness, " he writes, "think only perfect health, and detach from all appearances of illness in this world." This will generate a dynamic aura of wholeness which will saturate your being and animate your thoughts until you feel and breathe and give out nothing but well-being and wholeness.

We must always be aware of negative thoughts, negative energies which interfere with the natural flow of positive energy into our lives. This resistance is in our thoughts. Any thought of doubt or fear or anxiety is a thought that resists healing. These thoughts must be consciously pushed aside. Positive, optimistic, healing thoughts must be activated in their place. Such thoughts, that are energetic and in tune with wholeness and well-being, will allow good health to infuse your life.

Wise men tell us that on an average, a human being allows nearly 60,000 thoughts to run through his mind, every day.

Alas, for us, most of these thoughts are tired, impoverished thoughts that we think over and over again and most of them are negative and defeatist.

The mind is often compared to a garden. If you care for your garden, you nurture it carefully, you lavish attention on it and cultivate it with loving effort so that it blooms into a beautiful vision. But if you neglect it and allow weeds to take root there, the garden of your mind will become a cluttered, seedy, untidy place. Good health and well-being can never grow in such a garden!

The mind is an infinitely valuable gift that God has given us. People can lead successful, satisfying lives without hands, eyes or legs. The world's greatest living physicist, Stephen Hawking, is a living example of a great man, indeed, a genius, who has not allowed severe physical disability to daunt him or impede his reading and research. We can cite him as the perfect example of a sound mind that has transcended, overcome the disadvantages of an unsound body. However, the reserve cannot be true. For if a man loses his mind, he is as good as dead!

Guru Nanak Dev was asked by a disciple: "What is the value of a human being?"

By way of reply, the saint handed over to him a diamond. "Take this to the market and have it appraised," the Guru instructed him. "Do not sell it; just take it to every shopkeeper and get a price for it."

The disciple visited every shop in the bazaar. The first shop he went to, was a fruit seller's. The man took a look at the stone and said, suspiciously, "A dozen oranges?"

The next shop was the green grocer's. The man promptly offered four kilos of potatoes for the diamond.

The disciple decided to visit all the jewelers in the street. Each one came out with varying estimates; one thousand, three thousand, ten thousand rupees.

Finally, the disciple went to the best known jeweler in town and asked him what he would give for the diamond. The jeweler studied the gem for a minute. "You are foolish to sell this exquisite stone, my friend," he said finally, "Believe me, it is rare and priceless."

The disciple returned to Guru Nanak and narrated his experiences.

"I hope you have the answer now," said the Guru to him. "A human being determines his own value. You can sell yourself for a dozen oranges or four kilos of potatoes. Or, you can regard yourself as rare and priceless. It all depends on your own attitude to yourself."

Many men are in the habit of emptying out their coat pockets just before they retire to bed at night. The pockets are turned out carefully: coins, money, valuables are neatly put away. Useless bits of paper are discarded.

Let us empty our minds just as we empty our pockets. There are so many useless thoughts and worries we pick up during the day, a little resentment here, a slight irritation there, a few annoyances and even some guilt reactions. Every night these should be drained out of our mind, just as we drain dirty water out of a wash-basin by removing the stopper.

Negative thoughts throw toxins into the blood stream. Therefore, we need to constantly cleanse the mind of all negative thoughts, and replace them with positive ones.

The English word worry is said to be derived from an Anglo Saxon root which means to strangle to choke. How true it is, that worry chokes us – cuts off the air supply of hope and faith that are so essential for a happy, healthy, joyous life!

There are several psychiatrists who believe that many of us actually create illness in our own bodies. The body, they argue, is only a mirror of our thoughts and beliefs. As we think, so we become. Every cell, every tissue in the body responds to every single thought we think, every single word we speak. Thus continuous negative thoughts or a constantly scowling face generate patterns of disease.

Body and mind are inseparable. The mind is known to influence the heart, the endocrine glands, the nervous system, blood circulation and other vital organs. When the mind is affected by negative thinking, all these systems are also affected, leading to ill-health.

Thoughts are forces. Thoughts have power. Thoughts produce vibrations, which affect the tissues and the blood chemistry. Worry, anger, excitement, tension – all this can adversely affect the well-being of an individual. Take the digestive system, for example. It is a proven fact that anxiety and stress lead to acidity, ulcers and other more severe disorders. On the other hand, positive thoughts are healing, health-giving and vital forces. A happy mind is the greatest aid to a healthy body. By focusing on positive thoughts, we contribute to our own good health and well-being.

Mental alertness, self-confidence, freedom from anxiety and fear, and the ability to take things in your stride – that is all it takes to turn your thoughts into positive, healing forces! That is why people who are mentally healthy lead better and happier lives than those who are merely physically fit. People who are mentally alert and active, continue to lead useful and satisfying lives even in old age, when their physical health begins to fail them.

All of us are aware of the hygiene of the body. How many of us, though, devote attention to the hygiene of the mind? Fear, anger, worry and other negative emotions litter the mind. They induce morbid states and generate toxins which create diseases. The health of the mind affects directly, the health of the body.

How often have we seen people who age prematurely! Fear and depression seem to shrivel the skin. Stress and strain seem to turn people grey-haired overnight. Worry and depression make us lose vitality and inhibit bodily functions. On the other hand, cheer, optimism, generosity, and affection are elevating emotions that promote health.

I would not go so far as to say that all diseases, aches and pains are wholly imaginary, or that they exist only in the mind. However, I would accept that the mind can play a major role in our good health, and that it can actually speed up the healing process when we actually fall ill. There is an ancient proverb that tells us, "A merry heart does more good than any medicine." I would qualify this by saying that a merry heart does as much good as any medicine. A sick body reveals itself in a sick mind – and a sick mind makes good health impossible. Thus a vicious cycle ensues, with mind and body continually depressing each other, leading to chronic conditions of illness.

Many physical ailments like paralysis, chronic indigestion and debility have been known to be cured by the power of the mind and its positive thoughts – when all other treatments have failed. For truly health lies deeper than muscles, bones and blood. The cultivation of the right mental attitude is thus of paramount importance in sustaining good health.

There are very many people, who through their thoughts, draw to themselves calamities, misfortunes and ailments. Doctors today speak of a new disease called *symptomatic imaginitis*. A person has simple symptoms, and he begins to imagine that he has contracted a dreadful disease. I know a woman, who, if she gets a headache, begins to imagine that she has developed a malignant tumour in the brain. There is a man who, whenever he overeats, gets a stomachache and promptly concludes that he has cancer of the intestines. By giving way to symptomatic imaginitis we are actually drawing diseases to ourselves! Therefore, we need to be careful about our thoughts.

Positive thinking must become a regular habit with us. We must allow positive thoughts to diffuse down to the depths of our subconscious mind, so that they can begin to influence our pattern of thinking and our mindset. I have known healers who urge patients to direct positive thoughts on their disease-prone areas, so that pain may be relieved and positive energies flow into the affected parts.

To promote a sense of constant well-being, you can practice this exercise at night, before you fall asleep. Close your eyes, empty your mind of all negative thoughts and fill your consciousness with this single thought: "By the grace of God, I'm feeling better and better, every day, in every way. " Affirm this to yourself, and a sense of well-being and harmony will permeate your mind.

Repeat the exercise when you wake up the next day. "By the grace of God, I'm feeling better and better, every day, in every way." You will be amazed to find the difference this makes in your daily life!

The process of using the mind to heal and vitalize the body is now a matter of consensus among the medical fraternity. We cannot, of course, become immune to all illness. But should sickness strike you or someone you love, here are a few simple suggestions to release the Lord's power of health and healing.

1. Cultivate the habit of wholesome thinking. Do not dwell on the illness or pain. Picture yourself as whole, healthy and happy.

2. Say your prayers with a positive mental attitude: God is the Source of infinite power and energy. Your positive prayer will help to channelize His power and energy into your well-being.

3. Believe and affirm constantly that God made your body for health and wholeness: He has put amazing

powers of healing in our mind and bodies. When we cultivate the right mental attitude, the body will heal itself.

4. Always keep your mind filled with great life-affirming principles and words from the great scriptures: look up and think up!

6

OLD AGE IS IN THE MIND

Sometime ago, I was in Bangalore to address a meeting of business executives. Among those present at the meeting was a doctor. When the meeting was over, he came up to me and said, very politely, "Can I ask you a personal question?"

I said to him, "Feel free to ask whatever you will!"

He cleared his throat and said, "Will you be so kind as to tell me your age?"

I smiled and said to him, "Can you make a guess? Can you guess what my age must be?"

He reflected for a moment and studied me from top to toe. Then he said, "I may not be very accurate; but of this I am sure – you cannot be more than seventy years."

Some one who was standing next to me told him, "Dada is approaching 84!"

The good doctor was taken aback. "I don't believe it!" he exclaimed.

"That makes two of us," I said to him. "I don't believe it either!"

You are as old or as young as you think yourself to be! Youth is not a matter of age or years; youth is a state of mind. If your mind continues to be fresh, if your mind is always open, if your mind is ever receptive to new ideas, if you are ever ready to undertake new experiments in the great laboratory of life, you will continue to remain young forever!

Youth is not a matter of age; youth is not a matter of years; youth is a state of mind. Keep your mind fresh! Keep your mind open! Keep your mind receptive to new ideas!

There is a friend of mine in the US, who recently celebrated her 90th birthday. In a letter that she wrote to me, she said, "I am celebrating my 90th birthday, and I am looking forward to being old!"

The point she made was this: she always thought of old age as being ten years ahead of her! She wrote, "When I was eighty, I thought I would be old at ninety, now I think I will be old when I am hundred!"

Her words made me recall these beautiful lines from a poem by Robert Browning:

Grow old along with me;
The best is yet to be!

I read about another American lady, who is described as a delightful, charming person, who is always positive. At 94, she continues to remain friendly, cheerful and full of high spirits. They asked her, "What is the secret of your life?"

She replied, "The secret is a very simple one. It is my enthusiasm for life. And because I always think positive, I am positive!"

She paused for a while and then added, "Of course I owe a lot of my positive thinking to my boy friends!"

"Boy friends?" They stared at her in disbelief. "Do you have boy friends at this age?"

"You bet I do," she replied cheerfully. "They are my constant, faithful companions to this day!"

"Do tell us about them," her friends pleaded.

"I get up each morning with the help of my first boy friend. He is Will Power. I go out for a walk with my second boy friend Arth Ritis. Arth Ritis has been my constant companion for the last thirty years. My evenings are spent with Ben Gay – he is such a soothing presence!"

Here was a lady who was young in spirit! She was a woman of tremendous will power; she suffered from arthritis which can be painful and crippling – but she had learnt to look upon the affliction as a regular companion; and the pain-killing ointment Bengay, used widely in the US, had become her healing soothing friend too!

We cannot help admiring her attitude to life. It is attitude that counts! And so she continues to be young, even at 94.

There is an old song that goes – "A very merry un-birthday to you!" It tells us that each of us can have only one birthday in a year, whereas the other 364 days are all un-birthdays. So why not celebrate our un-birthdays rather than just our birthdays?

It has been rightly said that to a wise man, every day is a festival day. If only you can control your mind, keep your mind fresh, open and always be receptive to new ideas, you can continue to be young all your life!

There are people who ask me, "Where do you get the energy to work so hard? How do you manage to travel so widely at this age? Where does all the energy come from?"

My reply to these people is always the same. "My friends, the energy is not mine at all! It is the energy of God who has created me and continues to re-create me everyday. All I do is keep my mind open and receptive to that energy. Each one of you can do it too! Keep your mind open and receive the energy that flows from God and you will continue to be young all your life!"

On the whole our attitude to old age is rather negative. Formerly this was confined to the Western countries – but now, it is spreading everywhere. We see old age as a series of losses – as Shakespeare put it: "Sans teeth, sans eyes, sans everything." (sans = without). It is regarded as a headlong descent into nothing!

Commercials make us associate old age with grey hair, wrinkles, a stooped gait, slow movement, and slower reflexes. We are made to believe that age is taking something away from us. If you are just the body, this kind of descent would be correct. But as we have seen, we are not the bodies we wear!

The story goes that a hard working man died and went to heaven. When he met his Maker face to face, he asked Him outright, "Lord, what is the idea of making men old? Why do you take away our physical gifts one after the other – our strength, our stamina, our speed, our agility – until we are left in a frail and decaying body?"

The Lord replied: "Dear child, ageing is not a curse, it is a gift that I have bestowed upon you, so that you may become mature and wise, realize that you are not the body, that you do not belong to this world, but to me, your Heavenly Father.

The message of this story is indeed beautiful! The proverb says, "What I gave, I got; what I lost, I gained." We lose childhood to gain youth. We lose youth to gain adulthood. At every stage of life, we lose to gain.

Ageing may deprive us of physical prowess and energy. But it is a stage when we grow spiritually. We grow in maturity, wisdom, understanding, patience and tolerance. The loss is physical – but the gain is spiritual. Need I tell you which is greater?

Experts say that irreversible ageing i.e. loss of vital cells leading to gradual physical debility – starts at the age of 25 years! It is in the nature of all matter to change with time. Wood, rock, stone, soil – you name it, it disintegrates with time. So does the body. But what is ageing to the body can be maturing to the mind and spiritual unfolding for the soul! If you believe that you are essentially a spirit, ageing should not bother you!

Finding Peace of Mind

Are you in quest of peace?
Do not resist. Walk the way of acceptance.
An accepted grief,
like a crushed flower, exudes fragrance.

J. P. Vaswani

1
HOW TO HAVE
PEACE OF MIND

This morning as I sat in my quiet corner, I put to myself a question. I asked myself what it is that we are all seeking? We, who are treading the pathway of life, we who are engaged in different types of activities, what is it that we are seeking? If I were to put this question to you, and to many others, I know that I would get a variety of answers. Some would say that they are in quest of money, others would say that they are in quest of pleasures. Yet others would say that were seeking power, fame, name and earthly greatness and honours. So there are some who are drawn to the pursuit of wealth, others who feel drawn to a pursuit of pleasures and yet others who feel drawn to a pursuit of power.

But if I were to put to them another question – why is it that you are seeking that which you are seeking? You say that you are seeking money, what is the reason? The one answer that I would get from everyone would be, because we want happiness. Those that are in pursuit of money, of this yellow dust that we call gold, they would tell me that they are seeking money because they feel acquisition of money would lead them to happiness. And those that are chasing the shadow shapes of pleasures they would tell me, that they are doing so in the hope that pleasures will make them happy. Likewise, those that are in pursuit, very often senseless pursuit, of power, they too, would give me the same answer. They too would tell me that they are in quest of power because they think that power will lead to happiness. In its ultimate analysis my friends, we, each one of us, is in quest of happiness.. Everyone of us wants happiness more than anything else in this world. Not only every human being, but every creature that breathes the breath of life, the ant that crawls, the worm that creeps, the insect that flies, the bird that each morning sitting perched on a branch of yon tree sings its soulful melodies, everyone of us is in quest of happiness. Everyone of us wants to be happy. And yet so few are happy.

There is a little book that I love. I turn to it again and again for guidance and daily inspiration. It is called *Shri Sukhmani Sahib*. And in this book the author – the Guru whom I regard as a prince among martyrs of humanity- says that the king of all the world is unhappy. Even if they gave you kingship of the entire world, you would not be happy. In this world kings are unhappy and princes are unhappy. Ministers are unhappy and VIPs are unhappy. Millionaires and multimillionaires are unhappy. Think of that great king, Frederick the Great. It is by this name that he is remembered in history till today. Towards the close of his life, on a memorable occasion he made a significant confession. He said, "I am unhappy".

The whole world is unhappy. What is the reason? We are all walking different pathways of life. We are all in quest of happiness and yet we are all unhappy. The reason is that we are seeking happiness on the wrong track. What is the right road to happiness? Surely not the way of possessions and pleasures and power. Jesus said two thousand years ago some words which are not recorded in the gospel but which we have in some of the eastern books of Islam. Jesus is reported to have said on one occasion. "Nothing in the morn have I and nothing do I have at night, yet there is none on earth happier than I." Jesus, the man of utter non-possessions, Jesus who owned nothing beyond the shirt that he wore, and even that, he said, did not belong to him. Often he passed it on to someone whose need was greater than his. Jesus makes this marvelous declaration: "there is none on earth happier than I." What then is the way to happiness?

We have an answer to this question, given to us in that great book which I regard as the bible of humanity. We revere it as the *Bhagavad Gita*. In one place Sri Krishna, while speaking to his dear devoted disciple, Arjuna, says: "Arjuna you say you want to be happy. Let me give you the prescription for happiness." And the words that the Lord uses are *"Ashantasya kutaha sukham"*. The literal meaning of these words is, without peace of mind how can you be happy? Until and unless you have attained to peace of mind, until and unless there is peace in the heart within you, all the wealth of the world and its pleasures and its powers, its name and fame and earthly greatness will not keep you happy. Without peace in the heart within, you will feel restless, as storm tossed boats. The secret of peace, the secret of happiness is in this one single phrase: Peace of mind, *chitta shanti*. So it is that at the conclusion of every invocation of every prayer of the great rishis of ancient India we have these words, *Om shanti, shanti, shanti*. Shanti is the secret to happiness. Peace of mind is the secret to happiness and the practical aspect of the problem is how to attain peace of mind?

The answer is: Forget thyself. Do you wish to get happiness? To get happiness, you must forget yourself. In our pursuit of happiness we are all selfish and greedy. Therefore happiness eludes us as a shy bird. The more we run after it the more it runs away from us. Forget yourselves my friends, forget yourself and you will get true happiness. And one way of forgetting yourself is to go out and serve others.

At the entrance to the city of Pune from where I come,

you will be greeted by a 10 foot high statue of my beloved Master, Sadhu Vaswani. We, in love and reverence, call him Beloved Dada. Beloved Dada's statue stands there blessing all the passers by. And the pedestal, on which the statue stands, has on its four sides four great teachings of the Master. One of the teachings is: "do you wish to be happy? Then go and make others happy." As you forget yourselves in trying to bring happiness into the lives of others, you find, one day, that the happiness which went out of you has returned to you many fold. Remember, my friends, happiness moves in a circle. The happiness that goes out of you is sure, sure as the sun rises in the east, it is sure to return to you and will be to you as music at midnight. Forget yourself, bring joy into the lives of the joyless ones.

Let us try to do at least one simple act of service everyday. One simple act of service. If you cannot do anything else, at least smile. Your smile can work wonders. Bring joy into the lives of the joyless ones, give food to the hungry, give water to the thirsty, give clothes to the naked. And remember birds and animals too are our younger brothers and sisters in the family of creation. To feed them is also to give joy to the universe, the joy which is sure to return to you. Try to reduce your wants. Live on simple wants. Do not be guided by the opinions of others. Do not be tied to material things. Do not depend on material things.

The secret of happiness is not the number of things you possess, but the number of things that you can do without. And always remember that youth is not a time of life. Youth is not a period in one's life, but it is a state of your mind. It is the freshness of your outlook. You can be 70 years young as you can be 17 years old. You are as young as your faith, as old as your fear. You are as young as your hopes as old as your despair.

2
BURN ANGER

Anger is a wild fire, a forest fire which spreads from shrub to shrub, from tree to tree, consuming everything that comes its way. Anger creates a chain reaction. Someone gets mad at me; I must take it out on someone else, otherwise it will keep on seething within me. That someone else must have it out on yet someone else. And the chain reaction goes on! A boss gets angry at an assistant: the anger is not justified. The poor assistant can't hit back. All that anger keeps on seething within him. As he returns home, he lets it out on his wife. The wife lets it out on the maid-servant. The child lets it out on a street dog. And the chain reaction goes on. The fire keeps on spreading.

On the surface, we all are good and virtuous. But, within each one of us, there lie hidden so many weaknesses and imperfections. When we are angry, the worst elements within us are made manifest. Therefore, burn anger before anger burns you.

The very first lesson that was taught to every student in ancient India was: *Satyam vada, krodham maakuru.* Always speak the truth and never yield to anger! This is the teaching that needs to be passed on to every student: "Always speak the truth; and howsoever strong the provocation, never yield to anger."

If anger is such an evil thing, why did God create it? Anger was created so that we could be angry at our own selves – for we turn our faces again and again from the Light and become victims to lust, hatred and greed. Anger is a weapon which has been given to us for self-improvement. Instead, we direct our anger at others and degrade ourselves.

A woman complained to Sadhu Vaswani: "I have prayed to God, again and again, to grant me the gift of the new life, but He does not listen."

Sadhu Vaswani said: "Why don't you use the stick?"

The woman was shocked. "How can I strike God with a stick?" she asked.

Sadhu Vaswani said: "Strike yourself!"

Anger is a two-edged sword. There is a type of anger which drains energy and produces tension. There is another type of anger that is a positive and a creative life-force. There is a type of anger which is known as righteous anger. When it is my duty to be angry, and I become angry – that is righteous anger. A parent has sometimes to be angry with a child for the good of the child. A teacher has sometimes to be angry with a student for the good of the student. An employer has sometimes to be angry with an employee for the good of the organization.

Jesus got angry with the temple priests when he found them selling birds in the temple. In anger, Jesus said, "What have you done? You have converted my Father's House into a business centre!" This is an example of righteous anger. If you find a man molesting a woman or ill-treating an animal on the roadside, you have every right to be angry. Anger becomes righteous when you get angry to defend the rights of another, without any selfish motive.

When a person gets angry, he activates certain glands in the body. This leads to an outpouring of adrenaline and other stress hormones, with noticeable physical consequences. The face reddens, blood pressure increases, the voice rises to a higher pitch, breathing becomes faster and deeper, the heart beats become harder, the muscles of the arms and legs tighten. The body moves into an excited state.

If a man is given to anger, all these processes are repeated again and again, and the man is surely heading towards serious health problems. The cumulative effect of the hormones released during anger episodes can add to the risk of coronary and other life-threatening diseases, including strokes, ulcers, high blood pressure. It is, therefore, in your own interest that you learn to control – or, in any case, reduce - your anger.

Recent researches have proved that people who are easily prone to anger get heart attacks more easily than those that are not so easily prone to anger. It has been proved that when a person is calm, peaceful and happy, the digestive processes work normally. When man comes under the influence of anger, the digestive processes are paralyzed. Therefore, doctors recommend that you should be cheerful and in good humour when you eat. If you don't feel cheerful, it is better that you lay off from your eating. Stomach ulcers are caused by anger. They recur even after operations, if the resentment continues.

Anger affects the entire body, for anger is poison. I read concerning a mother who was given to frequent bouts of anger. Her infant received milk from her while she was in angry moods. Soon the baby died. Anger throws poison into the blood stream.

There are three ways of handling anger. There is, firstly, the way of expression. Psychiatrists tell us that it is good to express anger. Expression gives you relief, for you get some satisfaction at having given a piece of your mind to the other person. This relief, however, is temporary. Resentments build up again, and you are ready for another spill out. Gradually, anger becomes a habit; a time comes when you become a slave to anger. You are controlled by anger; and anger is a terrible master. I read concerning a mother. In a mood of anger, she threw her own child into the fire! Expression of anger is not the right way. Expression is very much like a cyst. You have it operated upon and get relief for some time; but the cyst gets filled up again, and you are in for another operation.

The second is the way of suppression. It, too, is not the right way. Suppression drives anger into the subconscious: there it works its subconscious havoc. Resentments that are pushed into the subconscious may develop into a complex and affect our entire behaviour and attitude towards life.

The right way is the way of forgiveness, of patience and forbearance. Forgive, and be free! Every night, before you retire, actually go over the happenings of the day. Has someone cheated you? Has someone offended you? Has someone hurt you or ill-treated you? Call out that person's name and say, "Mr. X, I forgive you!" You will have a peaceful sleep and beautiful dreams. The right way to overcome anger is the way of forgiveness.

I recall an incident in the life of the great Prussian king – Frederick the Second. One day, he found one of his servants taking a little snuff from his silver snuff-box.

"Do you like this snuff-box?" asked the king in utter simplicity.

The boy servant, realizing that he was caught in the act of stealing, felt embarrassed and hung his head low in shame. He did not answer.

Once again, the king repeated the question: "Do you like the snuff-box?"

The boy looked up and said: "Yes, sire, it is indeed a beautiful snuff-box!"

"Then" said the king, "take it. For it is too small for the two of us!"

Alexander the Great, as he was about to return from India, remembered that his people had asked him to bring with himself an Indian yogi. He set out in quest of one and found him sitting in a forest, underneath a tree, in silent meditation. Alexander went and sat in front of the yogi, in silence.

When the yogi opened his eyes, Alexander found that they were lit up with a strange light. He said to the yogi: Won't you come with me to Greece? I will give you everything you need. A section of the palace will be reserved for you. Servants will wait in attendance and do your bidding."

The yogi smiled. "I have no needs,." He answered. "I do not need servants to do my bidding. And I have no desire to go to Greece."

The point-blank refusal upset Alexander. He was enraged.

Unsheathing his sword, he said to the yogi: " Do you know, I can cut you into pieces? I am Alexander, the world conqueror."

The yogi smiled again and said quietly: "You have made two statements. The first is that you can cut me into pieces. No, you cannot cut me into pieces. You can only cut the body which is but a garment I have worn. I am immortal, deathless, eternal. And your second statement is that you are a world conqueror. May I tell you, you are only a slave of my slave?"

Intrigued, Alexander said: "I do not understand."

The yogi explained to him: "Anger is my slave: it is under my control. But you are a slave of anger: how easily you lose your temper! Therefore , are you a slave of my slave.!"

It is not individuals or situations that cause anger. It is one's own reaction or response to individuals and situations that determines whether we will be angry or otherwise.

3
THE QUEST FOR PEACE

Throughout the centuries, nations have sought many ways to attain peace. Many methods have they tried – force, aggression – yes! They have claimed that they have fought wars to bring about peace! They have also tried negotiations, conferences, treaties and 'peace' talks. They have had a League of Nations in the past, they have United Nations now. But where, O where is peace...true peace?

I believe peace must have three dimensions: peace within our own selves; peace among the nations; and peace with nature!

The first dimension of peace: peace within. What is peace? I may tell you what peace is in many words, but all descriptions will fail and you will not understand those words until you have felt peace in the heart within! Like love, peace must be felt!

One of the questions people ask me most often is: Do you think it is possible for anyone to lead a life of peace in these troubled times? My reply is: It is not only possible; it is your birthright. Yes, *ananda*, bliss, the peace that passeth, nay, surpasseth understanding is your birthright! You are a child of God – and he is the source of eternal bliss, unending bliss. The moment you realize that you are a child of God, you will let nothing affect you. All you need to do is forget yourself – and realize your true self as a child of God. When we forget this outer self, transcend the phenomenal, material world, we draw closer to the real, inner self, which is peace.

In Chap.2 of the *Bhagavad Gita*, the Lord gives us the wonderful picture of the *stitha prajna*, the balanced man. He says:

> A man with a disciplined mind, who moves among sense objects, with the senses under control and free from attachment and aversion, he rises to a state of *prasadam*, peace…Having attained peace, there is for him an end of all sorrow: of such a man of peace the understanding soon attaineth equilibrium.

> – Bhagavad Gita, Chap. II. vv.64, 65

These *slokas* emphasize the great truth that only a person who is not disturbed by the incessant flow of desires can achieve peace; not the man who strives to satisfy desires. These *slokas*, I am told, were very dear to the heart of Mahatma Gandhi. He had them recited everyday at his prayer meetings.

Yes, there is truly one way of achieving peace of mind and that is to attain the realization that all that happens, happens according to the will of God.

Why is it that we lose our peace of mind? Because our wishes, our desires, are crossed. We want a particular thing to be done in a particular manner. When it happens in a different way, perhaps in exactly the opposite way, our peace is lost. Why do we feel upset, frustrated, disappointed? Because we are attached, because we are involved. If I do my work, if I live my life as if I am plying role, I would not be upset.

If something happens in a play, do you feel upset? Supposing another 'character' in the play scolds you or speaks ill of you, do you get angry? No! You know you have to play your part well. If only we can realize this, that we are all actors in the drama of life; that the role you are playing has been given to you by the Cosmic Director – we will never, ever feel upset. We will not be entangled.

But, of course, there's a catch. In the cosmic drama of life, you have to play a double role. You have to be an actor and you also have to be a spectator. You have to watch the play unfolding before your eyes – and you also have to act. If you are able to do this, you will not lose your peace of mind.

It is not easy to do this – maintain your inner equilibrium at all times and in all situations. Sadhu Vaswani used to tell us, "God upsets our plans to set up His own. And His plans are always perfect."

If I have the faith that whatever has happened to me is according to the plan of the Highest, that there is some hidden good in it for me, I will not be upset! Sadhu Vaswani also used to say: "Every disappointment is His appointment. And He knows best."

Once you realize this, there is no more frustration, no more unhappiness. You abide in a state of tranquility and peace. You may not be able to achieve this straight away. It is a process through which you must move.

One way of attaining peace of mind, is to sit in silence everyday for ten to fifteen minutes, and explain this one thing to yourself. "Whatever happens, happens according to the will of God. If something happens contrary to my desires, it has happened according to God's will. Therefore, there must be some good in it for me." Explain this to your mind everyday. "O mind, why is it that you lose your peace?"

May I say to you, you will get peace of mind if you give your own "piece" to others. The great poet saint, Saint Tulsidas, says:

Tulsi is sansar mein kar leejiye do kaam
Dene ko tukda bhala, lene ko Hari naam

"Keep on giving", the saint tell us. "When you have learnt to give, you have learnt to live aright. Then peace automatically wakes up in the heart within."

It is only because we are so self-centered that our peace is disturbed. Peace is our original nature. We are made of peace. Each one of us is *sat chit ananda*. Ananda is the joy, the bliss that no ending knows. This is our original state – we have only to get back to it!

I am sure you must have seen on several occasions that when your mind is disturbed, and you do a little painting, or play a little tune, or sing a song, you find that peace fills you all at once. Why? Because you forget yourself in this creative work. Likewise, when we move out of ourselves and give joy to those who are in need of joy, we forget ourselves – we forget to be self-centered – and peace is ours! When we forget the outer self, we draw closer to the real, the inner self, which is peace.

We live in an excited, agitated world – a world beset with stress and strain. This intensified stress and strain manifests itself physically as heart disease, hypertension and nervous breakdown. Doctors agree that the cause of such ailments is psychological rather than physical. The great athletic trainer William Muldoon once said, "People do not die of disease, they die of internal combustion."

Our ancestors in India were fond of saying: "*Mann durust, tann durust.*" If the mind is at peace, the body is bound to be hale and hearty. It all sounds so simple and logical; with peace our minds are balanced, our bodies healthy and our hearts are happy. Life doesn't seem like a challenge anymore!

So let us move ahead to the discovery of true peace. Below are eight steps to interior peace.

Step 1: Begin the Day with God

Our tomorrows depend a great deal on our todays. And our todays depend on what we do with our mornings. The first thing we do on getting up in the morning shapes the entire day.

Every morning when you wake up, there is a choice before you: you can choose optimism, faith, positive thinking and right attitude; or you can choose pessimism, defeat, negative thinking and despair. What would you choose?

If you wish to have peace of mind, you must not take anything for granted. Therefore, remember to thank the Lord for everything – and thank Him everyday, first thing in the morning. And the very first thing you should thank Him for is the gift of a new day.

Even as you try to focus your mind on God, you will find a hundred thoughts crowding in. Most of them are not really useful or constructive. Therefore, after you have expressed your gratitude to God, let your mind dwell for a minute or two on a great thought – a great saying, a line or a *sloka* from the scriptures.

If you do this at the dawn of a new day, you will find that your mind is repeatedly drawn to this text during the course of the day. This will make a great difference to the state of your mind.

Begin the day with God. Take up a great thought of a great one and reflect upon it. Repeat this great thought whenever you can, throughout the day. And spend some time in silence every morning. You will find that you have made a sound investment for your own interior peace!

When we begin the day with god, we harness ourselves to the source of the highest power and energy in the Universe. We give ourselves the best start that we are capable of. We reiterate our utter dependence on God and ensure that He is with us in all that we do.

Step 2: Let Your Mind rest in God

Focussing on the Divine Presence is an excellent cure for a

restless mind. When your mind is restless, you can achieve nothing, you cannot concentrate on anything worthwhile, you cannot analyze your situation dispassionately; you cannot find a constructive approach to any issues; you cannot solve problems – in short, you cannot face the challenges that life throws before you and hence you cannot face life itself in a proper manner.

Resting your mind in the Divine Presence, as it were, focuses the mind, energizes and vitalizes your intellectual abilities so that you are able to give your best to the situation at hand. Many people tend to set apart work and worship. I believe there is a relationship between the two. The work should be done in a spirit of worship; when we worship, we need not neglect our work.

Step 3: Be a Lion, Not a Dog

When I was a school-boy growing up in Karachi, a holy man visited the city. I often went to sit at his feet and listen to his teachings. Once when I took leave of him, I said to him, "Baba, please give me a teaching."

Do you know what he said to me? He said, "*Sher bano, kutta nahi bano.*" Be a lion, don't be a dog

I was thoroughly bewildered. I said to him hesitantly, "Baba I think I am a lion, because I was born under the sign of Leo. But what do you mean by saying don't be a dog?"

The holy man explained, "If you throw a ball at a dog, what does the dog do? It runs after the ball! If you throw anything at a lion, he will ignore that object and go after you. He will go after the thrower, not the object that is thrown."

We are all the time thinking about what has been thrown at us, about circumstances and conditions in which we live, about the changing vicissitudes of life, the passing shows of life. We do not think of Him, the Thrower who has thrown all these things at us!

If you wish to think of Him, you must empty your mind of all else. So long as you hold worries and anxieties in the mind, so long as your mind is not empty you cannot think of Him – and you will not be at peace. Therefore, empty your mind of all worries and anxiety. Be like the lion, not like the dog!

Step 4: Don't Concentrate on Problems — Concentrate on Solutions

Problems are a mark of life, a sign of life. If you even have a day when you did not have to face a single problem, you will be well advised to read the obituary columns of your newspaper to find out if your name appears there. It is only the dead who don't face problems!

Problems do not come to us by accident. They are deliberately thrown in our way by a beneficent Providence for our own good. In the measure in which we handle these problems successfully, in that measure we will be able to unfold the tremendous powers of the Spirit, the immense energies of the eternal that lie locked up within everyone of us. If we are able to unfold even a fraction of these infinite powers, we would realize that there is nothing that we cannot achieve! And the best way to unfold, unlock these hidden powers is the way of handling problems and challenges in the right way.

The right way to handle problems is to look at the solution! The greatest satisfaction in life comes to you not in running away from problems, not in the dereliction of tough duties, but in meeting and solving problems, in facing up to challenges as a dependable, responsible individual.

There are three ways of meeting a problem but only one of them is the right way. The first is to run away from the problem. But it will come back to you with a vengeance.

The second way is that of passive resignation. This is also a negative approach although it is better than the previous way. The third way is the way of glad acceptance. Move forward to greet the problem. Life is a school and experience is our teacher. And every experience that comes to us has a valuable lesson to teach. So meet your problems, face them bravely and actually co-operate with them, knowing that they bring to you a rich treasure, a treasure which you must receive. This is a right way of meeting a problem. It is the way of acceptance, the way of victory!

Our life on earth is but a moment in eternity. When we learn to view our problems through the windows of eternity, we will find that they are so trivial, so tiny, that they do not affect us at all! When problems surface, insights disappear. When insights surface, problems disappear!

Step 5: Count Your Blessings

When you become aware of 'abundance' in your life, your attitude to circumstances will change and you will be ready to take on 'lean' and 'dark' days with a more positive and constructive attitude. This sense of abundance will add to your faith and contribute to your peace of mind.

The trouble with most of us is that we are so busy chasing after more – more money, more comforts, more opportunities – that we fail to appreciate what we have already! Count your blessings! And you will be filled with hope, optimism and faith that will help you face the challenges of life!

Step 6: Accept God's Will

Acceptance in the spirit of gratitude unlocks the fullness in our lives. It restores peace into our hearts and helps us to look forward to the morrow in the faith that God is always with us. It is not enough to speak of gratitude or enact deeds of gratitude – we must live gratitude by practicing acceptance of God's will in all conditions, in all incidents and accidents of life.

Wisdom consists in accepting God's will – not with despair or resignation, but in peace and faith, knowing that our journey through life has been perfectly planned by Infinite love and Infinite wisdom. There can be no mistake in God's plan for us!

Step 7: Do Your Best — Leave the Rest to God

The secret of inner peace is to work without attachment to the results of action. When you rid yourself of the desire to 'achieve' results, when you are free from anxiety and stress that arises from expectations, you escape the twin perils of egoistic arrogance on one hand, and dejection/depression on the other. If your efforts are crowned with success, it is His doing. If you should face failure, it is His will!

Avoid overwork! For it has been the graveyard of many a noble soul. The overworked man is a burden to himself and a nuisance to others. Do not rush through your daily tasks. Move slowly and quietly from one work to another, pausing again and again, for a brief while, to remember the Lord, to offer a little prayer, before you continue with your work.

It is not the *amount* of work we do that matters, but the *way* we do it; it is not *what* we do, but *how* we do it. Alas, many of us place too much dependence on ourselves, our efforts and endavours. We keep God out of the picture. Of course human effort has its place in life. But we need to understand that above all effort is His Will and His Grace. And He is the giver of all that is! So let us learn to work as His agents and He will take care of everything else!

Step 8: Pray Without Ceasing!

Prayer is a very simple matter. For me, it is just speaking with

God. He is with you everywhere. He is available to you at all times. You must remember too, that what is impossible with man is possible with God. Whenever you find yourself in a difficult situation, passing through a period of darkness, there is One who is always there with you. When you have done your very best, but are unable to solve the problem, just hand it over to God!

In the beginning you will find that prayer requires discipline and practice. But as time passes, the discipline becomes unnecessary because prayer becomes a part of your consciousness. After all, prayer is just a concentration of positive thoughts.

Praying ceaselessly is not a ritual; it is not about words or gestures. It has been described as a constant state of awareness of our oneness with God. You may of course, ask for all the good things you need – and you may, gain the faith that it is all obtainable to you. For all prayer is effective – but ceaseless prayer has multiplied effect.

4

WAKE UP!

Among thousands of men scarcely one sets out in search of God, says the *Gita*. Many of those who seek the Lord, alas! do not seek Him aright. I have heard a number of my brothers exclaim; "How I wished I lived far from the madding crowds of men, in the depths of a jungle or on the heights of a mountain peak!" They forget that it is not *where* they live that matters but *how* they live. It is not *where* they work but *how* they work. By this is not meant that all places and all works are alike. Surely, to meditate is better than to talk to people, and the sanctuary is a better place than the market. But wherever we are and whatever we do, let us maintain the same yearning towards God and equanimity of mind which cannot be perturbed. This will enable us to live and move and have our being in God.

Many believe that they will never be happy unless they are in a particular place or doing a particular type of work. And because their desires are not fulfilled they feel an inner restlessness and an urge to "escape" life which they misinterpret as spiritual awakening. Actually, it is not better than self-will. What I need to escape is myself, and no outer condition. When I think that this condition or that is a hindrance to my spiritual progress, I suffer from an illusion. What hinders me is myself, my attitude to men and matters. This, indeed, is the root cause of restlessness.

Spiritual life begins with forsaking oneself. "You are your own prison," says Pir Jamal. "Arise and quickly depart."

The cause of my restlessness is myself. Wherever I go, be it the highest heaven, so long as I carry the self with me, I shall continue to be restless. I can run away from places and outer conditions: but I cannot run away from myself. Until I have learnt to free me from myself, I can have no real rest and peace of mind. He who seeks peace in outer things and places seeks it in vain. The more he seeks, the further recedes the goal.

What then, should a man do? He must learn to abandon himself. He must practice the one and only renunciation – renunciation of the self. He who renounces himself renounces all things. Then, like King Janaka, he can live the life of a free man even in the comforts and luxuries of a palace. Wonderful are the words of the great German mystic, Meister Eckhart: "If a man has renounced a kingdom, or the whole world, and retains himself, he has renounced nothing. Indeed, if a man abandons himself, whatever he may then retain, whether it be wealth or honour, or whatever it may be, he has renounced all things."

True renunciation is not measured by the things a man gives up. True renunciation is of the will and of desires. A man may have ever so little of the goods and wealth of the world. Yet, if he has desires, he is attached to the things of the world. He desires them: he longs to possess them and, in that measure, holds them as his own. When, under God's grace, such a man learns the lesson of true renunciation – which is inner renunciation – he will have given up not merely the few things he actually possesses but all other things to which he clung in his desires. The man who renounces his all – be it ever so little – renounces the whole world. The renunciation of a poor man is no less than the renunciation of a king.

The life of self-abandon is the true life. In this you ask

for nothing, desire nothing, claim nothing, but accept all situations and circumstances with a heart that rejoices in the Lord. It is a life of child-like trust in the All-Loving Mother. She provides all the needs of Her Children. In several cases she provides even before the need is felt.

"Which book would you recommend to me for study?" a dear brother asked me the other day. And I said to him: "The book meant for you will come to you."

If only we knew that we were imprisoned in prisons of our own making! No outside force fetters us. Is it what we *say* and *do* that forges the chains which bind us mercilessly to the wheel of sin and suffering. If freedom is to be won, our entire life must undergo a change. For most of us such a task is impossible of achievement through our own efforts – unaided, alone. We need the help and guidance of an evolved Soul, a Teacher, an Inspirer, a Friend of God. No one else will help us. No one else *can* help us. There are many who will sympathize with us and even shed tears with us, but that will not give our distracted hearts the consolation they need. All true consolation comes from within.

We have set up wrong relations with people by thinking what we should not have thought about them, by saying what we should not have said about them. We have thought in terms of jealousy and hatred, of suspicion and scorn, of doubt and disdain. Let us start thinking the other way round! We have spoken words of disrespect and dishonor, of insult and abuse, of rage and outrage, of irreverence and affront, of mockery and ridicule. We have spoken words which have cut into the hearts of others, wounding them beyond repair. It is time we started upon the work of healing!

How often do we not enter into controversies when we had rather remain silent! All controversy is heat: and heat is pride. Controversy puffs up the ego and so throws barriers in

the way of self-realization. Who is right? Who can say? Let but each one walk according to the light that is shown to him. What is right for me may be wrong for another: what is right for him may be wrong for me. For though we all come from One and to Him must, one day, return, we all are so different from each other – in equipment, in opportunities, in heredity, in traditional background. Let us only be true to the Truth as we see it. If I know what is right for me, let me strive to live by it. I can never know what is right for another: he will know it himself and will shape his life in accord with it. No fighting over words, for words never reach Reality. The world will not improve by argumentation and hot discussion, but by radiating thoughts of love and compassion.

And how often do we not gossip about others, when we should be minding our own business? How often do we not, as Jesus said, see "the mote in another's eye," when we should be careful about "the beam in our own?" Our houses and our clubs, our hotels and our hostels, aye, even our offices and workshops are becoming, ever-increasingly, centres of gossip. Gossip, it has been rightly remarked, is spiritual murder. Many a promising life has been wrecked by gossip.

There is an inviolable law which governs the universe from end to end: what you send out comes back to you! Do you send out thoughts of hatred and enmity to others? Hatred and enmity will come back to you, turning your life into a veritable hell! Do you send out loving thoughts to others? Do you pray for struggling souls? Do you serve those that are in need? And are you kind to the passers-by, the pilgrims on the way who seek your hospitality? Then, remember, sure as the sun rises in the East, all these things will return to you, making your life beautiful and bright as a rose garden in the season of spring!

Has life been unkind to you? Do your brothers and sisters mistreat you at home? Do your friends forsake you and your co-workers pay little heed to your wishes? Do you get a cold reception wherever you go? Then, may I tell you, brother! What you should do is not find fault with others. But search yourself and see where you are at fault. The treatment you receive from the outside world is only a reflection of what is going on within you. He whose heart is a flowing fountain of love will be greeted with love wherever he goes. He who is harmless will be harmed by none.

This applies not to men only, but, also, to birds and animals, to all creatures who have the breath of life. In our daily life we may endeavour not to harm human beings: but alas! Our attitude towards birds and animals – poor, helpless, defenseless creatures of god - is one of cruel indifference. Else would we eschew meat-eating and wearing clothes which involve the murder of millions of little innocent insects – the silk-worms. Every shirt of silk, every silken sari is built in the death of a million creatures who have as much right to live as we have. Little wonder that with all the comfort at our disposal, we feel so unhappy.

In the day I achieve complete harmlessness in thought, words and deed, I shall have been free from all problems. That I still have problems is clear proof that I have not yet attained to the state of harmlessness. Let me start right now upon the task of renouncing harmful thinking and harmful speech.

What may I do? Let me first understand that in nine cases out of ten it were better for me to keep silent that to speak. Most of the words I speak are either useless or destructive in character. So let me make it a practice to pause before I speak and consider if what I am about to say is better than silence. I shall find that there will arise very few occasions on which it will be beneficial to break my silence.

5

THE PATH OF YOGA AND
ITS OBSTACLES

The path of yoga is open to each and every one of us. For yoga, difficult and cumbersome postures are not needed. Even Kapila and Patanjali, the great exponents of yoga, tell us that all we need is to sit in an easy, comfortable, stable and relaxed posture. Only see to it that the head, the neck and the spine are in a straight line.

Many people labour under the impression that *pranayama* is a technique that is difficult to master. I remember a lovely incident in the life of my Beloved Master, Sadhu Vaswani. He was asked, "Do you practice *pranayama?*" His reply was significant indeed. He said, "My *pranayama* is *Rama nama.*"

Sri Aurobindo, who has written and talked about yoga, does not emphasise the technical aspects. He stresses instead, that the consciousness must be lifted to a higher level. Sri Ramana Maharishi, the great sage of Thiruvannamalai, said to his disciples, "Why waste time on *asanas* and *pranayama?* Just lift up your consciousness!"

Our minds, alas, are scattered. They are dispersed – because they are tainted with desire. We need to purify our minds. The level of our consciousness needs to be raised. The seat of the mind is between and a little behind the two eyebrows. But the mind is looking downwards. We need to turn the gaze of the mind upwards. Therefore it is, that seemingly out of nowhere, impure thoughts wake up within our hearts.

We must be on our guard against three things that make our minds impure. They are the three obstacles on the path of yoga. The very first obstacle is love of pleasure; the desire for sense-gratification and sense-indulgence. Sri Ramakrishna referred to this obstacles as *kamini* – one whom we must guard against.

There is a fable about the bee, which found a pot of honey left near the hive. The bee thought to itself, "Now why should I labour all day, flying from flower to flower, gathering honey little by little? Here is a store of honey which I can reach easily – and its all mine!"

So the bee went into the pot and reveled in the honey. When it began to get tired and cloyed, the poor bee found that its wings and feet were clogged – and it could not drag itself out of the sticky mess of honey. The bee died and got buried in its own pleasure!

We are told that the Devil once called a meeting of all his associates. The forces of evil were all present at the meeting – each one boasting of his victories and conquests. Anger, envy, greed and jealousy were all boasting of their numerous victims. Soon a heated argument ensued: who, among them, could take the credit for wreaking the greatest havoc on mankind?

Impurity won, hands down. Conferring the dubious distinction upon him, the Devil himself remarked: "He is the one with the sharpest sword, the deadliest poison. All he has to do is to sow a single thought of impurity in the mind – it is enough to cause the greatest havoc."

I am reminded of my Beloved Master Sadhu Vaswani. When he was a student, he carried a pin with him. Whenever an angry or negative thought entered his mind, he would prick himself with the pin, so that the impure thought could be thrown out at once.

Following his example, I too, developed the habit of stopping every impure thought in its tracks. I would slap myself sharply, when such a thought intervened.

"Was that a mosquito?" my friends would ask me. "Yes – the deadliest," I would reply. For an impure thought is the deadliest and most infectious bite!

The second obstacle on the path of yoga is greed of gold – the desire to amass wealth. We all know the story of King Midas – he whose greed for gold was legendary. He obtained a boon from the Gods, so that all he touched would be turned into gold. He had a wonderful time to begin with! He touched everything around him and it turned to gold. His joy knew no bounds. Within a day, he was surrounded by as much gold as a man could ever wish for.

Tired and famished, he asked for a meal to be brought to him. No sooner did he lay his hands on the food, than it turned to gold. Bread, fruits, vegetables, whatever he touched, turned to gold. Which was all very well – but what could he eat? Gold could satisfy his greed – but it could not appease his hunger! A sadder, wiser Midas offered to return his boon to the gods – for he had learnt that gold could not bring him all that a man needed.

The third obstacle on the path of yoga is desire for power – desire for fame, name, publicity, popularity and earthly greatness.

How low a man sometimes stoops to gain power, position and authority! We would have no graft or corruption in the world today, were it not for such men. And then there is flattery, falsehood and hypocrisy which people adopt to please those in power. Such practices only point to the lowest self in man. These undesirable elements only taint our minds and hearts and impede our spiritual progress – which is the only progress that matters.

What is it that we seek through this power and glory? Where will they lead us eventually? To what avail is earthly greatness when we know that anytime the call can come for us – and we shall all be reduced to nothing more than a handful of dust and ashes!

To defend ourselves against the three pronged attack of *maya,* we need faith and willpower. For this, we must pray, again and again, to the Lord. In the *Gita* is unfolded a memorable picture of a tortoise. Once the tortoise draws in its limbs, you will not be able to drawn them out even if you cut the creature into four pieces. This is the kind of willpower we need to develop if we would wish to tread the path of yoga. Patanjali also lists nine *antarayas* or obstacles which we encounter on the path of yoga: he describes them as rocks which obstruct the path of the aspirant. These are:

1) Illness
2) Lethargy
3) Doubt
4) Hate or impatience
5) Fatigue
6) Distraction
7) Arrogance
8) Inability to proceed
9) Loss of confidence

These are manifested as physical symptoms as well as in a negative attitude to life.

1. Illness: Physical illness disturbs mind and body. One cannot undertake yogic practices in a state of ill-health.

2. Lethargy: Our mood has a direct bearing on our

minds. When we feel low and lethargic, we are under the influence of *tamas*, and we cannot do anything useful. This condition can be caused by overeating, eating the wrong kind of food or by cold weather.

3. Doubt or *samsaya* is a negative and persistent feeling which creates uncertainty in the mind. This can severely undermine our practice of yoga.

4. Haste, leading to impatience and rashness will cause us to slip instead of making progress.

5. Fatigue or exhaustion, known as *alasya* leads to negative thinking. Our confidence is undermined, and our energy is depleted. At such a stage we need to be remotivated to pursue our yogic practices.

6. Distraction or *avirati* impedes our concentration and leads us to temptation. We are led in the wrong direction and lose our concentration on yoga.

7. Arrogance is perhaps the greatest hurdle we must overcome. When we think we know everything, we lose ourselves in *avidya* – ignorance and illusion.

8. Inability to proceed – to take the next step – causes us to become disheartened. We feel that our goal is still too far, and we are inclined to give up our pursuit.

9. Loss of confidence makes us feel that we can neither maintain the position we reached, nor progress further on the path. As a result we fall back, losing whatever we have gained.

These are the obstacles we may encounter on the path of yoga. A good teacher can help us overcome these setbacks and put us on the right track once again. Even more effective is submission to the Lord's Will – *ishwarapranidhana*. God is the highest Spiritual Being –and surrendering to His Will, can only bring us the benefits of His blessing.

6
OVERCOMING IRRITATION

When we say 'irritation' or 'annoyance' we always associate these terms with trifles, petty issues, events and situations with what we call "nuisance value". So, you might ask, why do we have to take 'irritation' and 'annoyance' so seriously? Have we not agreed that they are, after all, trifling and petty?

A middle-aged housewife was asked to list all the things and events that added to her list of everyday irritations. She wrote down the following list:

1. The ringing of the morning alarm just when she is sinking into a deep and dreamless sleep.

2. Getting the family members up, one after the other, running around to get them ready for school/work/college/business.

3. The constant ringing of the telephone/doorbell.

4. Dealing with maidservants and the provocations they bring.

5. Waiting interminably for the bus/public transport.

6. Carrying a load of shopping bags home.

7. Cooking breakfasts/lunches/dinners and other meals day after day after day....

Taken individually, these are no doubt trifles. But taken collectively, they represent continous little snips and cuts which

will eventually make one's peace of mind and serenity wear thin. Minor or superficial they may be, they undermine your effectiveness and add raw, sharp edges to your personality. Before long, you begin to snap and lose your temper with your near and dear ones, and the petty annoyance you started with, becomes a veritable contagion! Our capacity for patience and tolerance is torn to shreds; and serenity and calm fly away from us!

When major crises and tough trials loom before us, we tend to tackle them with great courage, fortitude and resourcefulness. But when trifling irritations and constant frustrations bother us, we tend to lose our cool.

An executive was driving to work when a rash driver almost hit his car, overtaking him from the left. When they stopped at the next signal, the executive got down from his car to protest to the other about his rash driving. No sooner did he climb down from his car, than a speeding two-wheeler knocked him down! In the meanwhile, the signal changed to green, and there was a cacophony of hooting and horns, and people shouting at him and calling him names! The poor man was reduced to a nervous wreck!

Every year in July-August, flights from Mumbai airport are delayed or cancelled due to heavy monsoon rains. Every year, in December-January, the fog affects flights from Delhi airport. Hundreds of passengers queue up at the terminals, impatient with the delays and lack of adequate information. Sometimes, some of them lose their temper, abusing or even assaulting airline personnel.

Mind you, when there has been an air-crash or a hijack or similar crisis, people tend to behave far more soberly and with great self-control. But a delay in departure or a flight cancellation makes them fly off the handle!

One of my friends, who is a doctor, said to me the other

day that many of his patients come to him with sudden outbreaks of high blood pressure. Outwardly they are calm, quiet, dignified individuals. But inwardly the daily frustrations and irritations of life are taking their toll on these men!

Let us accept, irritations are inevitable in our daily lives. We will have to face them, tackle them and master them, before we get on with the daily business of life. If we are wise and mature, we will learn to handle them without paying a heavy price in terms of frayed nerves and acute emotions.

When we focus our mind constantly on irritations, we only allow them to linger on and become festering annoyances. The trick is to snap out of irritations and recover our calm and serenity. Better still, we should learn to block out irritations altogether, by adopting a tolerant, easy going attitude towards people and events.

Rahim was the assistant manager of the front office of a hotel. A lady had checked into one of the deluxe rooms. She was out all day, leaving at nine in the morning and returning only at eight p.m. She met Rahim once in the morning, when she handed over her keys, and once at night, when she collected them from the front desk. Each time she would shoot off a list of complaints and demands; she would fuss over the messages left for her and in general make life tough for him.

Rahim had been trained at an eminent institute and had obtained a diploma in Hotel Management. But he had to grit his teeth and put up with the lady, who was beginning to get on his nerves. He spoke to his mother about her one night, when he went home.

"Be patient with her, son, and send out a prayer for her when she annoys you," advised his mother, who was a wise and compassionate woman. "God knows what's bothering her, poor soul!"

Rahim decided to follow his mother's advice. For the next few days, he listened patiently to the lady, attended to her complaints promptly and arranged all that she wanted.

A week later she came down to settle her bill. "Please order a taxi to take me to the airport," she requested.

" I hope you found your stay pleasant and comfortable, Ma'am," Rahim said to her. "We do hope you will come back to stay with us whenever you are in this city."

To his shock, the lady burst into tears. "Oh, I hope I'll never, ever come back here," she said with a sob. "My former husband, who deserted me years ago to run away with another woman, was in the hospital, dying of cancer. He asked to see me, and I had to come here so that I could bury the bitter past and help him die in peace. But it has been too much for me! He is dead now, and I must go back and allow my own wound to heal!"

Rahim was startled to realize that while he had been battling with the petty irritation caused by her behaviour, she had been passing through a terrible emotional ordeal.

It is a tough, hectic, fast world in which we live. As they say, it's a rat race that is going on out there. But the worst part of being in the rat race is that even if you win – you are still a rat!

Once you refuse to give in to irritation and annoyance, you will find that the world is a different place altogether. All it requires is patience, tolerance, understanding and faith! Learn to have an objective, detached and dispassionate attitude to problems. Try to understand why some people behave as they do, and you will find that their behaviour no longer upsets you. Instead, you will find yourself sympathizing with them and trying to help them in anyway you can!

By giving in to irritation, we allow our energy levels to

drain; our efficiency drastically lowers; and we also lay ourselves open to worse problems that are sure to follow.

Have you seen the comic strip where an irate driver kicks the flat tyre of his car – and then howls in pain as his foot is sprained by the kick? Granted, it is a human tendency to want to hit back at whatever – or whoever – has annoyed you. But it can be an even more satisfying experience when you control your resentment and become the master, not only over yourself, but the situation. And remember, the man who can master a situation by self-control, always wins the battles of life!

Friends, every one of us knows what it is to feel irritated and unhappy. We are, after all, ordinary people and even great men have given in to irritation at one time or another! Therefore, we have to work hard at conquering irritations.

A mature, wise, tolerant and spiritual person learns to face life's daily irritations without being upset. Jimmy Durante, the comedian, schooled himself never to be upset, never to feel irritated. Whenever he was faced with a trying situation, he would exclaim, "That's the situation that prevails – so what can you do about it?"

A distinguished writer received a visitor at his house. The visitor wanted to look at the room where all his wonderful novels were written. The writer led him to his study. The visitor was shocked to find the room exposed to a veritable din of noise – noise from the traffic outside, a TV blaring from the flat next door, pots and pans banging about in the kitchen and so on.

"How can you work in here?" the visitor gasped in astonishment. "How can you concentrate amidst all this noise?"

The writer smiled. "The noise does not bother me," he said. "I cannot stop the traffic outside. I cannot dictate terms to my neighbours. We all have to eat – and the servant must do her work in the kitchen. When I want silence, I shut the doors and windows and turn on the fan. I know it's a one-way adjustment, but it works well for me!"

Patience is the formula which can help you black out, shut out every kind of irritation!

Malik Dinar was a Sufi saint. His neighbour was a Jew, who wished to annoy the saint constantly. He built his toilets just outside the entrance to Malik Dinar's house – so that whenever the saint left his home or came back, he had to cross a row of stinking toilets that were deliberately left unclean for days together.

The saint did not feel irritated or upset. Whenever he left his house or came back, he held his handkerchief across his nose, and moved away quietly. He never ever forgot to greet the Jew and bless him whenever they met.

"Don't you feel annoyed when you have to pass by my toilets every day?" the Jew asked him one day.

"Upset?" asked Malik Dinar. "What right have I to feel upset? I only have to cover my nose with a handkerchief – that doesn't take much!"

That was one-way adjustment too! When we learn this art of adjustment, we can turn every tragedy into a triumph. For, as I said, if your mind is focused on irritations, they will never leave you. Patience is the magic formula to conquer irritations.

How may we overcome irritations and annoyances? I would like to pass on to you eight practical suggestions. As I always say, you need not practice all eight simultaneously. It is enough if you adopt one or two of them and try to bear witness to them in deeds of daily life. You will also find that a different tactic is required to tackle different kinds of situations. Take them up, one at a time, and see how they may be put to work for your benefit!

1. Be Aware that God is always watching over you!

2. Always be relaxed in body and mind.

3. Do not neglect your daily appointment with God.

4. Always see the bright side of things.

5. Count your blessings.

6. Keep yourself busy doing something creative.

7. Smile, smile, all the while

8. Help others!

THE CAUSES OF STRESS

Modern life and stress seem to go together. The way we live, the way we work, the way we talk, the way we function everyday, contribute to the building up of stress. People rush about all the time, as though they were carrying the entire burden of the world upon their shoulders. People rush about, accumulating what they think they need – only to realize that they don't need it at all. They resemble squirrels in a cage – running, running all the time – but getting nowhere.

We seem to be in a hurry all the time! It is not only when we are on our feet that we are hurrying; when we are seated, at rest, our minds are rushing somewhere or the other. We may be waiting in an outer office, waiting for an appointment with a doctor, waiting for an interview call – but we are hurrying, rushing our thoughts. This mental rush, this mental hurry is one of the main causes of tension.

We need to take it easy! Take it easy my brother! Take it easy, sister! There is a word which Spanish people use often. Whenever two Spaniards meet, they say to each other, "Tranquilo! Tranquilo!" Tranquilo means – take it easy! This is the message which all of us need today – Take it easy! Take it easy!

A white man once saw a black man sitting underneath a tree. The white man disapproved of the black man, for he felt that he was wasting time.

"What are you doing Tom?" the white man asked him sternly.

"Why sir, I'm just enjoying myself", Tom replied.

"Why don't you get up and work, Tom?" the white man said to him in a tone of disapproval.

"What for?" Tom wanted to know.

"If you work hard, you will be able to earn money!" explained the white man patiently.

"But what for sir?" Tom persisted.

"If you make money, you can save some of it."

"What for?"

"If you save money, you can have plenty of leisure."

"What for?"

"If you have leisure you can go out on a holiday."

"What for?"

"If you go out on a holiday you will be able to enjoy life."

"But sir," exclaimed Tom, "that's what I'm doing already!"

We don't have to be lazy like the man in the story – but at least, we must avoid needless hurry. As the proverb tells us, "Haste makes waste." And a lesser known Spanish saying warns us: "He who pours water hastily into a bottle spills more than goes in."

Haste and rashness are like storms and tempests which break and wreck people's lives and their businesses. How much do we lose out on the little joys of life when we cannot walk, talk, think or listen slowly!

Another cause of stress is irritation. We give in again and again to irritation. We may not always show it – but the irritation inside burns up our emotional energy uselessly. Every time you are irritated, you are burning up valuable emotional energy, which can be used constructively. We must develop the patience to curb irritation. A Dutch proverb tells us: "A handful of patience is worth more than a bushel of brains." Wise men like Benjamin Franklin would agree: "He that can have patience can have what he will."

Yet another cause of stress is that we are overwhelmed by the problems we face. I always say that problems are wonderful presents that are thrown at us by Providence – only, we fail to recognize the gift because it comes wrapped up in a soiled package. The word 'problem' is derived from the Latin word "pro balo" and means that which is deliberately thrown in our way. It is because we react to problems negatively that we create panic and stress within us.

It has been said that a problem is like a pebble. If you hold it close to you eye, it seems magnified, and it blocks your entire vision. If you hold it at arm's length, you can see its shape, its colour and size. If you drop it at your feet, you can effortlessly walk over it!

Another reason why we react negatively to stress situations is mental fatigue and exhaustion. We are often apt to underestimate the demands of intellectual or mental work, as against hard, physical labour. Psychiatrists say that people who work with their brains need more sleep and rest than manual workers. When mental fatigue sets in, we cannot think clearly or react reasonably.

Picture to yourself a man sitting slouched on a sofa. His shoulders are drooping. His head is down, and he is holding his chin in both his hands. His entire body seems to be drooping. Is not this the condition of many of us at the end of a day's work? What a weary burden we have made of a day – which has been God's brand new gift to us just a few hours ago?

A man went to his Guru, complaining of utter fatigue and exhaustion. "Swamiji, I just cannot cope any more," he complained. "Please help me!"

The Guru took him to an inner chamber, where there were two clocks on the table. Both were ticking away merrily. One was a freestanding clock; the other was connected to the mains with a power cable.

"This clock will keep going for less than 24 hours," said the Guru, pointing to the first one. "After just one day, it will slow down and begin to lose time gradually. I have to come in every morning and wind it up to keep it going, or else it will soon come to a stop."

He pointed to the electric clock. "This one you can see, is connected to a source of high power and with the energy from that source, it keeps going, on and on. It does not need to be wound up every day. It just goes on, ticking merrily."

The man stared at the two clocks, unable to understand what the Guru was saying.

"You must connect yourself to God – the source of the highest, purest and best energy in the Universe," said the Guru. "Then you will not have to be pushed from outside. No one will have to wind you, or give you a boost. You will draw all the energy and wisdom of the Universe through your connection with God, and nothing can stop you!"

The world looks bleak and miserable to those who are fatigued. Give the body enough sleep; recharge your heart and soul by connecting yourself to God constantly. Then, your soul can work to relieve your stress and restore your depleted energy.

Rediscovering
the Joy of Living

Who is the truly happy man?
Not he who has many things, but he who
can do without them.

J. P. Vaswani

1

BE LIKE LITTLE CHILDREN

Our difficulties and dangers begin the moment we cease to be children. When I think I have grown up and I am able to look after myself, I am faced with trials and tribulations which overwhelm me, again and again, and which rob me of the joy of living. The child is singularly free from worries and cares, for it knows, beyond a shadow of doubt, that the mother is there to provide for all its needs. The mother anticipates the needs of her children and provides for them well in advance. We, who think we are independent, only create for ourselves a situation in which we have to slave from dawn to dusk. True freedom belongs to the child!

A 'child-soul' I met many years ago. He was advanced in years and age had written wrinkles in his face, but the smile of God was in his eyes. And he always looked fresh and radiant as a child of five.

And I said to him, "Sanat Kumar! O youth Eternal! Tell me, what is the secret of your unsullied freshness?"

And he answered: "I always feel fresh, for I have no worries, no cares, no anxieties."

And in sheer wonderment, I asked, "Do you mean to say that no unpleasant occurrence has ever crossed your path?"

"Far from it," he answered quietly. "The basket of my life has been filled, again and again, with many a bitter fruit.

Failures and frustrations have come to me in and out of season. But they touch me not. For when I find myself in an unpleasant situation, I enter within myself and, gazing and gazing and still gazing at the calm, beauteous countenance of the Mother Divine, say to Her, 'Ma! Mother! Here is one more burden for you to bear!" And then I forget all about it. And all goes well with me, always!"

The strong alone can shoulder the burden!" So sings the beloved poet of Sind. Our tragedy is that we try to lift heavy loads on our weak shoulders, when we can so easily pass them on to One to whom all the burden of the universe is as a feather's weight. Weighed down by burdens we cannot and need not carry, we move through life, travailing and groaning in agony and pain. All we need to do is to go within ourselves and make contact with the Mother Divine and cast our cares at Her Lotus-feet. Then we may well move along the pathways of life, singing as we go!

Be still to know they God! All around us is the sorry spectacle of restless men, moving on from one work to another, achieving nothing, knowing not whither they move. To them all speaketh the word resounding through the centuries, "O children of an agitated age! Be still! Be still!" To be still, is to be relaxed, is to be restful. Avoid overwork! Overwork is the graveyard of many a noble soul. The overworked man is a burden to himself and a nuisance to others. Do not rush through your daily tasks. But move slowly and quietly from one duty to another; pausing again and again, for a brief while, to pray and rest at the Mother's Lotus-feet. "This work, O Mother Beloved! Is Thine. May I be but an instrument of They Will Divine!" This aspiration has the power of transforming the most secular work into a sacrament. This aspiration keeps the contact alive and makes our work a source of blessing and inspiration to all who cross our path.

The world today, wanders from unrest to unrest. Men and women alike, in the East and the West, await a new outpouring of the spirit, a new illumination, a new revelation of the Heart. It will flow not through the so-called great ones, but through the little ones, the children of God.

One mark of the childlike soul is that he hath no care for the morrow. He is singularly free from all fear of the future. Who will feed me tomorrow? Who will supply my daily needs? Such thoughts do not beset his mind. For him it is enough that the Mother *is*! She will provide. It is Her sole responsibility to take care of us and look after all our needs. The little child playing in your compound has not the least anxiety about his mid-day meal. His mother is there to provide at the right time.

Of Guru Amardas, it is said, that each evening he gave away all he had, keeping not a grain of corn for the morrow, not a copper coin in his purse. Before night fell, he emptied his store of provisions; he even drained the pitchers dry! "The morrow will take care of itself!" he said to his disciples who wondered at his strange behaviour. And the morrow did take care of itself. The Guru was not an ascetic, he was a family man with wife and children. Each day he had a *langar* (common kitchen) at which many a pilgrim and passer-by ate their fill. Unshakeable was the Guru's faith in providence, and providence never failed him.

Of Jesus it is related that pointing to a procession of ants, he said to his disciples, "Ye of little faith! Look at the ants, who gives them their daily food?"

And one of the disciples said, "Master! They need so little!"

"Then look at the birds!" said Jesus. "They toil not nor do they save for the morrow. Yet they get their daily food and are happy!"

And the disciple said, "Master! Birds have wings with which they fly and pluck fruits from trees!"

"And what about the wild beats?" Jesus asked. "How fat they are! They have no wings. Yet they too, get their daily food!"

The child of God does not take life "seriously". He understands that all that happens is but a play of the Mother divine. He becomes the Mother's playmate, accepting all that comes to him cheerfully, meeting all situations merrily. He does not prepare in advance. He does not make any plans. He but lives as a child of the Mother, and he knows that in the measure in which he becomes a willing tool in the Hands of the Mother, the Great Plan will be revealed to him. So he claims nothing; he asks nothing; he seeks nothing; he plans nothing; he becomes a channel for the divine plan to flow through. To such a one death loses its terror and defeat and despair tastes sweet. In pleasure and pain, in loss and gain, he gives gratitude to God.

The child of the Mother rejoices in the darkest hours of life, and becomes a bearer of the torch to many. He seeks no honour for himself but readily gives it to others. He flatters no one and he fears no one. He feels happy in occupying the lowest place, in doing the meanest task. He feels no responsibility and he seeks no reward. But in the depths of darkness, when not a star doth shine, he lifts up his tear-touched eyes and beholds the sweet smile on the Mother's Face and hears Her still, small voice say, "Well done, my child! I, thy Mother, am not afar! I am with thee, within thee!"

Convert work into yagna (offering to the Lord) and you are linked with the Lord. The light shines in your life if you connect yourself with the Great Light, God, through yagna, self-offering; a new power will course through your body and you will speak as spake the apostles of Jesus on the day of Pentecost!

2
LAUGH AS MUCH
AS YOU CAN!

I am convinced that many of our problems can be solved, if only we relearn the gift of laughter. The tragedy of modern man is that he does not laugh enough. Laughter, I always say, is a powerful tonic – it vitalizes the body, mind and spirit. It is an excellent dry-cleaner – it cleanses you from inside.

There is something funny about all of us – sometimes ridiculous, sometimes even absurd! Each one of us has his faults and failings, his quirks and oddities. So learn to laugh at yourself first. When you learn to laugh at yourself, you will never be offended when others laugh at you.

There was a famous orator who was invited to lecture at the Dublin University Hall in Ireland. On the day that his public lecture was scheduled, it rained very heavily in Dublin. Many people stayed away and the auditorium was practically empty. Naturally, the orator was upset. When he began his lecture, he cast a sour glance at the scattered audience and said to them, "Do you know that I am a famous orator? I have addressed large audiences at International Conferences, at the UNO and at the House of Commons. I am also a famous playwright, a distinguished thinker, a luminous intellectual…." And he went on and on with the list of his achievements. He ended it all by saying, "But the pity of it all is that *I* am so many and *you* are so few!"

Do you know that there is a very popular movement called the Laughter Club which is spreading rapidly all over the world? Its founders believe that "laughter has no language, knows no boundaries and it does not discriminate between caste, creed and colour. It is a powerful emotion and has all the ingredients for uniting the entire world." I could not agree more! Truly has it been said: laugh, and the world laughs with you!

The holistic benefits of laughter have been well researched and well documented. Laughter relaxes the muscles, expands the blood vessels, improves circulation and reduces the level of stress-causing hormones. Above all, laughter exercises your facial muscles, improving your 'face value'!

It has been calculated that it takes forty-two muscles to frown; and a scowl causes lines and wrinkles to form on your skin. Whereas you use just seventeen muscles to smile – and it reduces wrinkles and tightens your chin and makes you look younger. So what will you choose – a scowl or a smile?

It was Victor Hugo who said, "Laughter is the sun that drives the winter from the human face." When you feel sad, depressed, tense, just look at your face in a mirror. It seems so serious, so constricted, so tight that you will not want others to see it! The stress and strain reflected on your face is obviously due to negative emotions that are playing havoc inside you.

Cheerfulness is the new wonder drug. Doctors tell us that our blood molecules contain receptors which receive signals from the brain. When you are happy, cheerful and contented, the receptors transmit these signals of happiness and the healing process within you is accelerated. Indeed, modern medicine assures us that if we laugh more, we grow healthier! Many doctors are convinced that if a man is happy and light hearted, disease will not draw close to him – and even if it does, it will not stay with him for long.

Did you know that many of the great ones of humanity

were also lovers of laughter? Socrates, St. Francis of Assisi, St. Teresa of Avila, Sri Ramakrishna Paramahansa, Sri Ramana Maharishi, Baba Ramdas, Mahatma Gandhi and Sadhu Vaswani, – to name but a few – all of them possessed a wonderful sense of humour.

Mahatma Gandhi said, "If I didn't have a sense of humour, I would have committed suicide long ago!"

Baba Ramdas said, "I did not have to shed tears. I laughed my way to God."

Sadhu Vaswani had a sparkling sense of humour. He could sometimes make us burst out in laughter. I remember one day, a doctor-friend who thought very highly of himself, came to him and said, "I have decided to give up my practice and devote all my time to the service of the country."

Sadhu Vaswani said to us, "I am not sure if he has given up his practice or his practice has given him up!"

People sometimes ask me very solemnly, "Dada does God ever laugh?"

My answer to them is: yes, God does laugh! He does not laugh at our weaknesses or imperfections, our heartaches and failures. But He does laugh at the ungodly world which thinks it can efface God out of existence. God also laughs when some of us remark that they can teach God how to make a better world. I find it amusing that many people swear that they wish to serve God, but they all want to serve Him in an advisory capacity!

God laughs too, when two brothers quarrel over the land and say to each other, "This land is mine and that is yours." God laughs, for He knows that everything belongs to Mother Earth.

One morning it began to rain heavily as William Dean Howells and Mark Twain came out of church after the Sunday service. Howells gazed at the sky anxiously, and asked his friend, "Do you think it will stop?"

"It always has," was Mark Twain's simple reply.

I am told that laughter has indeed become a 'serious' business these days! Laughter Workshops and Laughter Leader Training programmes are being held all over the world. People are also being taught "the underlying philosophy" and the "skills" of different kinds of laughter.

My advice to you is, "With or without the theory, learn to laugh! Laugh at yourself. Laugh with others. Laugh your way to health and harmony!"

Here is what Sri Anandamayi Ma tells us:

Whenever you have the chance, laugh as much as you can. By this, all the rigid knots in your body will be loosened. But to laugh superficially is not enough; your whole being must be united in laughter, both outwardly and inwardly....what you usually do is laugh with your mouth, while your mind and emotions are not involved. You must laugh with your whole countenance, with your whole heart and soul, with all the breath of your life...you will then see how the laughter that flows from such a heart defeats the world!

Laughter, especially the ability to laugh at oneself, is the greatest gift we can have. For humour tempers our faith, even as carbon tempers iron, to produce a tougher, more resistant substance.

ACCEPT! ACCEPT! ACCEPT!

Imbibe the spirit of acceptance. Accept all that happens to you as the Will of God. By accepting all that happens to us in the right spirit, we are settling the accounts of our previous karma, and making sure of good karma for our future. There are so many things in life that we cannot understand or come to terms with; the loss of a loved one, a sudden illness or an unexpected accident. Instead of wasting our time and effort on the why and wherefore of such events, let us accept them in the spirit of surrender. For we must never ever forget that we are only reaping what we have sown. When we accept life's incidents and accidents in this spirit, our sorrows and sufferings are considerably mitigated. On the other hand, if we try to resist them or defy them, our misery only deepens. Fighting pain and sufferings with egotistic rigidity serves no purpose. Ultimately, this kind of rigidity will break our hearts and minds.

There is a beautiful story told to us in the *Mahabharata*. It is said that the god of the Ocean once said to the River Ganga, "O Ganga! You bring with you huge banyan and oak trees as you flow into me. Why is it that you don't bring me some of those tender, delicate herbs that grow on your banks?"

The Ganga replied, "Those tender herbs you speak of may appear frail and weak, but, even though my water sweeps over them with force, they only bow down low before me, allowing me to flow past. Oaks and banyans, on the other hand, stand up against my flood, and I break them by their roots."

Egoistic defiance will only break you. On the other hand, humility and acceptance will give you the strength to resist adversity. If you bend, you cannot be broken! Accept! Accept! Accept! When you cultivate the spirit of acceptance, you move towards the goal of *samata* or equanimity. *Samata* implies balance, serenity and tranquility, which are born out of spiritual understanding. And, therefore, Sri Krishna declares in the *Gita*: *samatvam yoga uchyate* – Equanimity is called Yoga.

When you lose your inner balance, you allow the world to overwhelm you, conquer you. When you retain your mental balance, you emerge the winner, even in the most trying of circumstances. It is not adversity, but also prosperity that topples our sense of balance. When we meet with success repeatedly, we grow egoistic and arrogant. We tend to overlook God's grace and develop a false sense of superiority.

Adversity on the other hand, brings out the worst of our negative emotions – fear, despair, misery and insecurity. We lose all sense of objectivity, and succumb to self-pity.

Thus, when we lack equanimity or the spirit of acceptance, both prosperity and adversity lead only to misery and disillusionment. Let us, instead, cultivate the spirit of humility in good times and bad times. Remember, every event, every incident is a reflection of God's mercy. It is His omnipotence that confers upon us both prosperity and adversity. Both are needed to help us unfold our spiritual strength. Both can prompt us towards good karma. When we accept all that happens to us as God's Will, we learn to live and act in the true spirit of a karma yogi.

Prosperity and adversity don't come to us by chance. They are the effect of our own karmic attainments. But both conditions can prove positive and helpful to our spiritual progress, if we turn to God in the spirit of acceptance and surrender. When we face adversity in the right frame of mind, we gain will power, patience, determination and detachment. All great achievers will testify that it was because of their adversities that they evolved towards greatness. Thus negative karma need not be a stumbling block for us!

Equally, prosperity is not something to be complacent about. We can make use of it to help others, serve suffering humanity, and learn to become selfless; we can utilize our leisure and good fortune to devote time to reflection and meditation. Saint Kabir emphasizes this when he says: "Everyone turns their mind to God in adversity, but not in prosperity. If one were to turn to God in prosperity, there would be no room for adversity!"

Acceptance of God's Will should not be passive and helpless – but joyous and positive. In fact, we should learn to praise God and thank Him for His infinite mercy, because He knows what is best for us. One of my favourite prayers is this:

Thou knowest everything Beloved!
Let Thy Will always be done!
In joy and sorrow, my Beloved,
Let They will always be done!

It has been said that the greatest saint in the world is not he who prays or fasts the most; nor even he who gives most alms; but he who is always thankful to God, who receives everything as an instance of God's goodness, and has a heart always ready to praise God for it.

William Law tell us, "If anyone would tell you the shortest, surest way to all happiness and perfection, he must tell you to make it a rule to thank and praise God for everything that happens to you. Whatever seeming calamity happens to you, if you thank and praise God for it, you turn it into a blessing. If you could work miracles, you could not do more for yourself, for with this thankful spirit, you will turn all that you touch into happiness!"

4

CONQUER FEAR

Fear is one mark that characterizes us, children of a skeptical age. We are afraid of the future, afraid of poverty, afraid of unemployment, afraid of dishonour and disgrace, afraid of disease and death – it seems to me that sometimes, we are afraid of life itself!

Fear is at the root of all our problems. It is the starting point for all evil. Fear gives rise to all our misfortune. Living in constant fear saps our vital energies, leaving us too drained and exhausted to savour the joy of life. Fear paralyses the mind, even as a stroke paralyses the body. It strikes at the nervous system; it causes stress and tension. It undermines our well-being. Worst of all, it robs us of happiness and destroys our peace of mind.

It was Marie Curie who said: "Nothing in life is to be feared; it is only to be understood." Alas, many of our fears are imaginary. There are people who live in a permanent state of anxiety. They will not be able to specify what they are afraid of. They just suffer from persistent apprehension about something or the other. They are afraid that something terrible will befall them sooner or later – though they will never be able to tell you what it is!

Imaginary fear, the fear of the nameless, causes havoc in people's lives. Some time ago, a rumour spread like wildfire across the United States that a white powdery substance capable of causing anthrax was being secretly dispersed all over the country. The fear psychosis that this rumour generated was tremendous. People became distrustful of all white substances – like talcum powder, common salt, castor sugar, etc.

Why is it that a vast majority of us live perpetually in fear of something or the other? Perhaps one reason is that we are lonely. The deepest tragedy of modern man is his loneliness. In spite of an ever-increasing number of clubs, hotels, restaurants, parks, museums, and theatres, people feel lonely and lost. This sense of loneliness leads to a feeling of frustration and many of us begin to feel that life is not worth living. Loneliness burdens the heart of people, sapping their strength, eating into their vital energies. Little wonder then that heart diseases are on the increase. Hypertension is a common ailment, even among the young. Nervous breakdowns are taking a heavy toll.

Fear is a poison that quickly circulates through the entire system, paralyzing the will, producing queer, unpleasant sensations in the mind and the heart, and sometimes causing unhealthy conditions like ulcers, acidity and fainting fits. Fear is a great foe of man. It must be uprooted before it overpowers you!

To live a full life, to live according to God's plan, to live life purposefully and meaningfully, requires courage. Life demands of us that we live with courage. Winston Churchill considered courage to be the greatest of all virtues, because we cannot exhibit any other virtue without it. Without the courage to act, justice would be impossible. Without the courage to love, compassion and understanding would not exist. Without the courage to endure, faith and hope would not flourish!

Linguistic experts relate the English word courage to the French word 'coeur', meaning heart. Courage is born of the heart. It is the heart's response to the impulse of fear. Tagore's

immortal hymn beings with the words: *Where the mind is without fear....*

Where the mind is without fear, that is where the land of freedom lies. For fear and freedom cancel out each other. If you are afraid, you cannot be free. And courage can liberate you from the clutches of fear.

For those of us who live by our faith, as well as those who place their beliefs on science, life poses a series of unanswered – at times unanswerable – questions. Why do bad things happen to good people? Why did a young, intelligent man, husband, father, brother and son to a family of wonderful people have to die of a rare, unheard of form of cancer? Why are beautiful young babies sometimes born blind or deformed or spastic? Why are the nations of this world piling up a nuclear arsenal that can destroy the planet ten times over? Truly it has been said, to be sentenced to life is to be sentenced to death! Therefore, it is said, cowards die several deaths.

Life is full of uncertainties, the unknown and the unknowable. The *Bhagavad Gita* tells us:

> *Meet the transient world*
> *With neither grasping nor fear,*
> *Trust the unfolding of life*
> *And you will attain true serenity.*

The uncertainties of life have to be taken on, in the spirit of acceptance. Escape and running away are no solutions. It was Helen Keller who said:

> "*security is mostly a superstition. It does not exist in nature, nor do children as a whole experience it. Avoiding danger is not safer in the long run than outright exposure. Life is either a daring adventure or nothing.*"

People often think that fear is a destructive emotion. This

is not entirely true. When we are afraid of things that truly threaten our security, such fear is protective. In fact, I would go so far as to say that man is fortunate to have learnt to fear certain things – or else, the human species would have been wiped out long ago.

Let us admit – fear is natural to human beings in many situations. It teaches us to be cautious. It fosters our sense of self-preservation. It helps us create safeguards for ourselves. It is what keeps us safe and secure.

Fear and anxiety are similar – but there is one crucial difference between them: the cognitive component of fear, which is recognizable to us by perception or reasoning. It is the expectation of a clear and specific danger. On the other hand, anxiety is vague and unspecific. "Something awful may happen to me!" "Something terrible is about to happen!" is the typical reaction of anxiety or panic disorder. Fear is based on reality, or an exaggeration of a real danger. Anxiety is based on an irrational or formless danger.

Fear permeates all aspects of our life on earth. There are two options open to you. One is to submit to your fears, allow yourself to be overwhelmed by them, making your life miserable in the process. I'm afraid very many people adopt this course. They live with their fear all their lives, suffering needless misery and anxiety. What a great pity this! The other option – the wiser alternative – is to conquer your fears, with God's help. When you do this, you achieve a remarkable victory that can change your life. This victory is not the prerogative of the holy, the mighty and the brave. All of us have the potential to achieve it.

Fear is a tenacious beast. It is like a potent poison that quickly circulates through the entire system, paralyzing the will. And fear is a merciless master. It is one of the greatest foes known to man. Overcome fear the moment it raises its head – or it will overpower you! Strike fear with the weapon of the spirit – the word of God. Utter the name that is dear to you – Krishna, Rama, Shyama, Jesus, Buddha, Allah, Nanak. Utter it again and again! Utter it in childlike faith and He whom you call will surely rush to your aid.

The spoken Word has the power to fight all evil – temptation, sin, anger and fear. This is why many people learn to recite a sacred mantra. A *mantra* is not just a word – its profound sound vibrations have the mystic power to align the mind and harmonize it. We believe that these sacred *mantras* were first heard in the divine consciousness of our ancient Rishis as they sat in deep meditation. Since then, these *mantras* have been handed down to the generations by great spiritual masters, for the benefit of all humanity. By repeating these *mantras* constantly, you will create beautiful positive vibrations within yourself – positively influencing your physical, emotional, intellectual and spiritual well-being. The *pranava mantra*, the cosmic sound which we represent as Om, has multiple aspects of divine vibration. In fact, many wise men feel that all *mantras* are only different facets of Om.

Many Gurus give a particular *mantra* or *naam* for their students to recite and meditate on. But there are also general *mantras* which all of us can repeat – such as Om, Hari Om, or Om Shanti. If you are not able to recite a *mantra*, you can recite a poem or a prayer which will sustain your strength and help you conquer fear. I know many people who have received strength and solace from that immortal hymn, *Abide With Me*.

Mohandas Gandhi was extremely timid and fearful as a child. The slightest noise would scare him: a shadow falling in the darkness would fill him with fright. He would not even go from one room to another in the night. The maidservant who took care of him said to him one day, "Mohan, why are you so afraid? Don't you know that Lord Rama is always with you – guiding you, guarding you, watching your every step and protecting you at all times? Whenever you are afraid, just repeat His name. He is all powerful. He will look after you!"

Young Mohandas began to repeat the sacred *Rama nama* from that day onwards. He found that his fear vanished like mist before the morning sun. The young boy grew up to be the great-souled leader who defied the might of the world's greatest colonial power. Fearlessness and moral courage enabled him to lead his country to glorious freedom. Ultimately, he faced the bullets of an assassin with the sacred *Rama nama* on his lips! Mahatma Gandhi, the apostle of non-violence taught us that *ahimsa* was also *abhaya* – fearlessness.

Fear is a tenacious beast that clings to the intricate webs of your consciousness. How can you free yourself from its clutches? The first step is to become aware that fear, like all other human weaknesses, is removable. It was not put into you by God. You acquired it somewhere along the way: you took it on yourself, or it was put into you by the environment in which you live. Whatever it was, *fear is removable.* The important thing is for you to realize that you are not condemned to live with fear all your life. It is removable! Once you realize this fact, you can begin to work on the process of actually removing it. This is possible through self-discipline.

Fearlessness is the first essential condition for spiritual growth. Sri Adi Shankaracharya, one of the greatest intellects of all time, urged that he who would walk the way of the spirit must have *vajrahridaya* – a heart strong as a thunderbolt.

When Swami Vivekananda returned from America and entered upon his work of regeneration in India, the one message which he delivered to the people as he traveled from town to town, from village to village, in this ancient land of heroes and sages was this: "Stand up, Be bold! Be strong! Strength is life, weakness is death. Weakness is the one cause of suffering. We

become miserable because we are weak. We lie, steal, kill and commit other crimes, because we are weak. We suffer because we are weak. Where there is nothing to weaken us, there is no death, no sorrow."

Freedom from fear is achieved through perseverance, tenacity and sheer will power. The yearning for freedom – political, social, intellectual, economic, racial or religious – is imbedded so deeply in men, that people even risk their lives to achieve it. This is the reason why *abhaya* or fearlessness, has been the hallmark of the world's greatest intellects, martyrs and saints. This was why Socrates drank hemlock, calmly and dispassionately. This was why Christ allowed himself to be crucified. This was why Mahatma Gandhi faced his assassin's bullets with the name of the Lord on his lips. These great souls had cultivated the will to be unafraid, the will to conquer fear at all cost.

"People do not lack strength," said Victor Hugo, "they lack will." We must never underestimate mind-power, the power of the will. Freedom from fear – as well as health, happiness and harmony – depends on thought-habits. Truly has it been said that even happiness is the product of habitual right-thinking. Therefore cultivate the will to be unafraid.

More often than not, the worst fears come to us not from the outside, but from the mind within. By asserting your will power, by changing your mind, you can change your life! When you sweep the inner kingdom of your mind free of negative feelings, you can eliminate even the fear of death. You can assert your will power to eliminate self-destructive behaviour. You can assert your will to create tranquility and peace all around you.

Alas, we are ready to place our faith in wealth, power, strength and intellect. But the giver of all these is God, and if we cannot place our faith in Him, then our own lives are truly lost. The Persian poet Saadi put it across boldly: "I fear God, and next to God I fear, most of all, him who fears Him not!"

Often, many of us behave as though God is dead. I recall how several years ago, something happened which threw me out of fear into the slough of despondency. I was sad, dejected and depressed. I met my Beloved Master, Sadhu Vaswani. He looked at my wretched face but once; he did not look again. Nor did he speak to me a single word of comfort. He behaved as if he had not seen me. Living under the same roof, I was denied the privilege of seeing him, whom I loved deeply. I could not understand what I then took to be Sadhu Vaswani's cold indifference. The old man who resides within everyone, whispered to me: "Now you know how much he loves you!"

It took me five days to realize that I must be of good cheer before I could be worthy of being admitted to Sadhu Vaswani's presence. Putting on a forced smile, I went up to him and asked for his blessings. He was as loving as ever. As he enfolded me in a warm embrace, unbidden tears rolled down my cheeks. He spoke to me affectionately, as though nothing had happened. I realized what a blunder I had committed by appearing before him with a sullen face.

Many months later, Sadhu Vaswani spoke to me of St. Francis, of the sufferings he had to face. St. Francis never renounced the smile on his lips. He was free from melancholy. He looked cheerful. He retained his sunny serenity and his humour. To his brothers he said, when laying down for them the rules of discipline: "Ye shall take care that ye do not behave outwardly like melancholy hypocrites. But ye shall behave in the Lord, fresh and gay and agreeable!"

The sweet, serene, bright face of St. Francis has been one of the inspirations of my life. I have meditated on it, again and again – and on his love-lit eyes. Often, I have recalled to myself one of his wonderful saying: "To the devil belongs to

be sad, but to us ever to be glad and rejoice in the Lord." St. Francis was an apostle of spiritual cheerfulness. He was never mournful and he was never afraid.

Fear freezes the spirit. Faith thaws it out, releases it, and sets its free – so the wise men tell us. I repeatedly tell my friends that fear is the child of unfaith. Fear and faith cannot exist together. When fear knocks at the door of the heart, send your faith to open the door, and you will find there is no one there! Faith gives us a life-saving connection with God, in whatever circumstances we find ourselves. Faith is always on the shore, holding a rope out to us; when we take hold of it, we are sure to be hauled to safety. And when we have faith in god, we cannot despair of our fellow human beings either! Faith in god will reinforce our faith in fellow human beings and help us understand life and overcome our weaknesses.

Many of us say our prayers, we profess faith in the Lord; we call upon Him to pilot us safely across the *sansar sagar* to the other shore – but we fail the test of faith during crucial moments and give in to doubt and despair. What we need is the kind of faith that will never fail us, the kind of faith that makes us realize that all things are possible to those who believe in His mercy and goodness.

When we are tormented by needless fear, when we are crushed by the blows of fate, we should turn to God in absolute faith and trust. When we link ourselves to Him, we allow positive energies to flow into our lives. Helpful, healing, wholesome thoughts come to us during periods of stillness, prayer and meditation. Fear often leads to extreme nervous tension. It is only through a relaxed nerve-consciousness that we can feel the healing power of God flowing into us. When our nervous system is in disharmony, it is impossible for god's harmonious, healing health-giving power to bring help and relief to our troubled minds.

When our minds are haunted by fear, the waters of the soul are muddied. We need to retreat, so that the soul may be refreshed. And where else can we find such an untroubled retreat as in the quiet depths of our own soul? If the soul is to be cleansed, we need to take a dip in the waters of silence – for silence is a great healer.

Within every one of us is a realm of peace, power and perfection. Through practice, we can, at will, enter this realm and contact God. When we do so, we become conscious of infinite power, a wondrous peace, and a beautiful sense of serenity within.

The first step to this inner serenity is relaxation. Alas, most of the time, we are tense without even realizing it. Even when we go to sleep, our body and mind are not relaxed: the fears and tensions of the day persist in our subconscious mind and we fail to enjoy restful sleep. So we wake up the next morning with a feeling of fatigue and mental exhaustion. We do not feel fresh and strong to meet the challenges of the new day. This goes on day after day; the tension and fear keep accumulating, until they manifest themselves in one physical illness or the other. So many diseases of the present day – heart attacks, high blood pressure, nervous breakdown, migraine, asthma – are due to this built-up tension. So much so, it is now being said, "People do not die of diseases: they die of internal combustion." We need to relax – relax in the consciousness that we are in God's presence, so that His healing power may flow into us.

Man is constantly given to worrying about the future. What does this anxiety do for us? It may not empty our tomorrows of sorrow, but it will certainly empty our today of its strength. And if the future should bring problems with it, this fear makes you unfit to cope with those problems. Therefore, it has been said, "Worrying about the future is like a rocking chair. It will keep on moving, but will not get you anywhere!" Such

needless fear is like the advance interest you pay on troubles that may never come your way!

God has endowed us with the health and strength that we need. He has blessed us with the means and resources to tackle our life each day, as it comes. He gives us the strength and courage to face each day, each moment of our lives. Why then should we trouble ourselves over the future?

I tell people again and again: you should not make yourself miserable, by thinking of the past or of the future. The past is a cancelled cheque. The future is just a promissory note. The present is the only cash in hand – so use it wisely and well. Make the most of the here and the now!

How many of us break our backs to provide against dangers that never come! How many toil to lay up riches which they never enjoy; to provide for exigencies that never happen; to prevent troubles that never come; and they sacrifice present comfort and enjoyment in guarding against the wants of a period they never live to see!

Give your best to the present! Concentrate on the task you are doing. Let all your energy and attention be focused on the present moment. When you follow this simple suggestion you will find yourself free from fear and tension. Truly it has been said, "A day of worry is more exhausting than a day of work." Honest work seldom hurts us. Nobody has been known to have been killed by hard work. But fear, stress and worry can be fatal.

An ocean liner is built in such a way that the captain can, at the touch of a button, lower massive steel doors that separate water-tight compartments in the bulkhead from one another. If the hull of the ship is breached in a disaster, this arrangement can still keep the ship afloat. In the voyage of our life too, we must learn to bring down the doors that shut out the past with all its errors and failures. Equally, we must also shut out the unborn future, so that we may live in the present. When we close the doors that shut out the past and the future, we will ensure that the ship of life sails smoothly ahead!

5

HOW TO HAVE REAL
FUN OUT OF LIFE

Fun, is this not what everyone of us wants? Every human being is in quest of happiness and fun. Everyone wants to be happy. Not merely every human being, but every creature that breathes the breath of life. The ant that crawls on stone, the worm that creeps, the insect that flies, the animal in the forest, the bird that sits on a branch of the tree singing its soulful melodies. Every creature that breathes the breath of life, desires to be happy. There is no creature that does not want to be happy.

Since the dawn of creation, man has been in search of happiness and this search has continued down the long corridors of time. And during the course of centuries, man has found that riches vanish, that fame is fickle, that honours and earthly greatness are fleeting, that success is an illusion. Where then may we find happiness? Where then may we have real fun out of life?

There is a parable about three men. Three men set out in quest of happiness. In their hearts was this one question: where is the secret of happiness? We want to live a truly happy life. We want to have the maximum fun out of life. So, one of them, after pondering over the question, arrived at the conclusion that fun lies is in the life of pleasure. I must have pleasure, he thought. I must have as much pleasure as I can get, for there is no fun without pleasure. He was a rich man. So he built for himself a beautiful palace and furnished it beautifully. The costliest carpets covered the floors of the rooms of his palace. There were wonderful wall hangings and paintings. It was a beautiful palace fully equipped and there this man led a life of comfort and luxury. He ate the most delicious food, and he drank the choicest of wines. To his court came the wise men from the different parts of the world for he enjoyed their discourses. To this palace came musicians and painters and artists, for he was a lover of beauty and song. He came in contact with the most beautiful women in the world, with the most charming women in the world. He pursued pleasure. During his young age, he found that there was some fun in pleasure; but as he grew in years, he arrived at the discovery that within every pleasure, there lurked a seed of pain. He made the discovery that the life which is given over merely to the pursuit of pleasure, ends in boredom. He felt tired of pleasure and when he was about to die, he said, "I am unhappy. I have not found real fun in the life of pleasure. I have not found true happiness in pleasure."

Who led a life of greater luxury than Prince Gautama, who later became the Buddha and showed the way to true happiness, to true fun? He showed this way to multitudes and he continues to show the way to millions upon millions of humanity. Prince Gautama was the only son of King Sudhodhana. The king loved his son more than he loved his own life and for the sake of fun, he built three palaces: one to be occupied during the summer, another for the winter and the third in which the prince went and lived during the rainy season. Prince Gautama was brought up in ease and comfort. He had everything that the world could give. He was married to the most beautiful and most charming girl in the land, the Princess Yashodhara. And to both of them was born a son whom Gautama named Rahul. The word Rahul means 'fetter'. Gautama thought, this son is a fetter for me who wants a life of freedom. So one night, when everyone was asleep, Gautama renounced his palace and moved out as a wandering mendicant, as a fakir in quest of the secret of happiness.

Where is the secret of happiness? Friends, as I said, the first man in the story found that true fun is not in the life given to pleasure. Now what did the second man do? He felt that pleasure is transient, pleasure is ephemeral; it is a bubble that bursts. And he said to himself, not for me the life of pleasure. I shall withdraw myself from the world. He thought that true happiness lies in the life of withdrawal from the world. It is in the life of withdrawal into oneself. So he cut himself off from the world and went to dwell on the peak of a holy hill. No one could reach him. He could reach no one. He dwelt in utter solitude. But he too did not find true happiness because a life which is lived in loneliness, cut off from all human companionship, is a barren life. It is barren as the sands of the desert. The life without love is barren and dry as the dust. The hermit's life is not the real way to happiness. It is not the way to a life of joy and peace, of fun and happiness.

Now what did the third man in the story do? The third man avoided both extremes. He thought not for me the extreme of pleasures, not for me the life of the hermit. I shall walk the middle path. And this third man thought that where there is no battle, no victory can be won. He said to himself, I shall live in the world but I shall not be of this world. So he began to lead a life devoted to duty: duty to God, to his fellowmen, to his family, to his community, to his country, to his nation; duty to humanity and duty to brother birds and animals. He believed that creation is one family and birds and animals too, are man's younger brothers and sisters in the only family of creation. He did his duty by all and he gave his love to all – to men, birds, animals, butterflies, ants and insects. He gave his love to trees and flowers, to rivers and rocks, to stars and streams, he gave his love to all creation. And he found that wherever there was love, there was abundance of fun. He did not shun pleasure. He enjoyed those simple innocent pleasures which his life unfolded to him and he did not shun a life of solitude. Everyday, he spent sometime in silence. Everyday, especially early in the morning, in the darkness of the dawn, he spent some time in silence when he communed with the wonder that is ageless, the wonder that is radiant in the sun, the moon, the stars, in every atom and in the *atman* within. Everyday he spent some time in solitude. Going apart from men he would ponder on the mystery of this endless adventure of existence. And when the time came for him to pass away, there was a beautiful smile on his lips and his last words, his parting words were: "I die a happy man." And those that were around him also exclaimed, here was a truly happy man.

The lesson of the parable is so obvious, friends, that it is superfluous to emphasize it. Yet very few take it to heart. We find so many in the world today trying to seek fun in a life that is given over to pleasures. Remember, behind every pleasure, there is a seed of pain. And we find so many who shun the paths of pleasure to go and live as hermits in solitude. They too, do not get the true experience of happiness, they too do not get real fun out of life, the real life. The way to have real fun is to live a life which is devoted to duty, a life of love and sympathy to all.

Today so many complain that life is not worth living, that life has no meaning, that there is no fun to be got out of life. So many feel frustrated with life. It is as though we are entering into an age of gloom. It is true, we live in an age of advancing science. Today man has reached a zenith of technological brilliance. Today man stands on a planet of limitless promise. He has probed the secret of the atom, the depths of the seas, the mysteries of his own mind and body. Yet, is he not sure of his own true purpose and being. He is faced by a terrible loneliness and his heart is beset by a thousand fears which he cannot name. Science has not shown to man the way to be happy.

I recall an amusing incident in the life of the great Russian scientist, Maxim Gorky. He once stood before a huge gathering of Russian peasants and spoke to them about the glories of science. He said, "look what science has done to you. It has taught you how to fly in the air like a bird and science has taught you how to dive into the sea like a fish." Then it is that a simple unlettered peasant got up and said: "Sir, what you say is true. Science has taught us how to fly in the air like a bird and how to dive into the sea like a fish. But science has not taught us how to live on earth in peace and harmony with fellowmen." This is what science has not been able to teach us and it appears to many all over the world that we are entering into a new age of gloom.

Arnold Toynbee the great historian, writer of those wonderful volumes on the study of history, was gifted with many insights. Somewhere in his writings, he says that industrial civilization has given us many benefits but we have received those benefits at a very heavy price. What is that price? That is peace of mind. We have been robbed of our peace of mind. We have lost the way to happiness, we cannot have real fun out of life. Living in this industrial age, we should be able to find out some way of having real fun out of life.

What is the way? I would pass on eight practical suggestions. I refer to them as the eight notes of the happy life. The musical scale has eighty notes, isn't it? *Sa re, ga, ma, pa, dha, ni sa.* Even so there are eight notes of a truly happy life. It is not necessary for you to put into practice all the eight practical suggestions at one and the same time. It is enough if you take up one of them. Choose any one that you like and try to put it into practice.

Suggestion No. 1:

If you want to have real fun out of life, put an end to all the fun-killers that you carry about with yourself, wherever you go. Some of these fun-killers are hatred, anger and fear.

There was a man who met me some years ago. His face was dark as charcoal. And he said to me, the fire of hatred is burning within my heart. And this fire will not be quenched, until I have shot the man who indirectly killed my father. There you are! Hatred is the fire and so long as the fire continues to burn in your heart, how can you have real fun? "Hatred ceaseth not by hatred" said the Buddha. "Hatred ceaseth by love."

Remember, friends, love is stronger than hatred even as light is stronger than darkness. You may have a room which has been in darkness for thousands of years. Just kindle one single matchstick and there will be light. Darkness will not say, "I have dwelt here for a thousand years, give me at least a hundred years to go out of this room." Darkness will vanish immediately. Light is always stronger than darkness. And love is always stronger than hatred.

I remember how the wife and children of an evil man would come to Beloved Dada's *satsang* every evening for comfort and solace. And this wicked man, one day came to Beloved Dada and showed his fist at him, at this saint of God, at this servant of suffering humanity. Showing his fist he said to him: "If you only knew how much I hate you!" And Beloved Dada looked lovingly at him and said gently, "Brother, if you only knew how much I love you!" The man stopped short. With tears in his eyes, he fell down at Beloved Dada's feet and begged for forgiveness. His life was transformed. He became a new man. And every evening along with his wife and children, he came to Beloved Dada's *satsang*.

The second fun-killer which you must exterminate is resentment. So long as you harbour a feeling of resentment you cannot have true fun. Yet another fun-killer is fear. All these fun-killers must be exterminated before you can have real fun out of life. If you find that you do not have real fun out of life, remember, there is some fun-killer lurking somewhere within your unconscious self.

Suggestion No. 2:

Put an end to the habit of thinking negatively, of talking negatively.

A businessman met me some months ago and showed me a card. On it were written the words, "Today, I shall not think one negative thought. Today I shall not speak one negative word." And this businessman told me that everyday, as he gets up in the morning, the first thing he does is to write those words anew. Friends, you must give up this habit of thinking negatively, of talking negatively. We often exaggerate our misfortunes. Did I not say that we must not anticipate troubles. For we anticipate so many troubles which never come to us.

Suggestion no. 3:

In every little thing that you do, pour the love of your heart: love for God and love for people, love for brother birds and animals, love for nature, love for yourself. Remember where there is love, there is lots of fun.

We often believe, mistakenly enough, that there is a lot of fun in teasing others. Once when Beloved Dada was a professor, he took his students out on an excursion. When they arrived at the place where they had to go, they found a number of labourers doing their work. The labourers had taken off their shoes and left them at a distance. And what did the students do? They took the shoes of the labourers and hid them thinking that they would have a good laugh when they witnessed the consternation of the labourers later on. Beloved Dada came to know of this. He came to them and said, "Come, I will show you how to have greater fun, better fun. Bring those shoes back. Put them back where you took them from and in each shoe, insert a rupee coin. Then go and stand at a distance and watch the faces of the labourers when they return.

The students did so and as they watched the astonishment on the faces of the labourers at the discovery in their torn shoes, their own faces beamed with joy. The students understood that there was greater fun in giving love than in teasing others.

Suggestion no. 4:

See the good in everyone. Remember, there is not a human being on earth who does not have some good in him or her. And this good each one of us has to emulate. Everyone who comes on earth comes to teach us. Do not see the faults and the vices of others.

It was the great Prophet of Iran, Bahaulla, who said to his disciples, "If ever you see in a man nine virtues and one vice, forget the one vice and think of the nine virtues. And if ever you see in a man nine vices, nine faults and only one virtue, think of that one virtue and forget the nine faults and you will be richly blessed!"

Take the differences between the personalities of Yudhisthira and Duryodhana. Yudhisthira and Duryodhana both studied in the ashram of Dronacharya. When they were little, Dronacharya once called Yudhisthira and bade him go out into the town and meet different people. He was then to return with the information of who was the worst of men that he had seen. Thereafter, Donacharya called Duryodhana and said "My child, go out to the town, meet different types of people and come back and tell me who is the noblest of men that you have met."

So both Yudhisthira and Duryodhana did as they were told. When Yudhisthira returned in the evening, Dronacharya asked him which was the worst man that he had met. Yudhisthira replied, "Master every man I met I found some good in him which I lacked. I had to learn some good from every man. I returned convinced that I am the worst man on earth." When Duryodhana returned, he was asked by his teacher who was the noblest man that he had met, and he replied: "Master, I went and met so many people but in everyone I found some fault which I do not possess. I have returned convinced that I am the noblest of men living on earth. This was the difference between the two. Yudhisthira was always happy, whether in the middle of the forest, in exile, and even when he was asked to abdicate the throne. Duryodhana, on the other hand, was always unhappy.

Suggestion No. 5:

If you would have the real joy out of life, don't remain idle for a single moment. Keep yourself busy all the time. The best and noblest of all action is to bring comfort to the comfortless, joy into the lives of the sorrowing, struggling ones. The happiness we give to others comes back to us. Happiness moves in a circle. The happiness that moves out of us flows back unto us.

A doctor related to me an incident which I cannot easily forget. He was once called to see a pale, sad, seventeen year old girl. A number of physicians had examined her and were unable to arrive at a diagnosis. They said that she was a psychological patient. When my doctor-friend saw her she lay on a sofa in a small room which was filled with silk tapestries. Her eyes were half-closed, her head was bowed and she was pale like a marble-statue.

The doctor easily guessed her sickness. She suffered in her gilded cage because she had never gone out to give happiness to those in need. The doctor asked her to get ready to go out with him and her father.

'With you?" asked the girl. "Where?"

In an undertone the doctor said: "That is my secret. I can only tell you that it is for your good and that of your father."

The girl got ready and the doctor took her and her father to a quarter where poor people lived. They took with themselves many things in cash and kind. At the first house which they visited, the doctor had to help her to keep her balance, as she walked to the second, she went ahead of the doctor. At the third, she almost ran. When the children kissed her hand the poor women thanked her, both she and her father cried for joy. That outing seemed short to her. And everyday, she searched for those whom she could make happy. She attained health, joy and happiness, which were not found in her palatial home but in the broken cottages of the poor to whom she gave the service of her generous heart.

Those of you who are frustrated with life, who feel unwanted, useless and bored, try this same medicine, and there will be no end of real joy for you.

Beloved Dada said to us:

"Did you see him on the road?

Did you leave him with the load?"

On the road of life are many who carry loads on their weak shoulders: and the loads are not merely physical. As you bear the loads of others, you will find that your hearts are filled with a wondrous feeling of happiness and joy.

Suggestion No. 6:

In everything that you do, pour the best that is in you. Whatever be the task that you are handling, pour into it the best of which you are capable. The smallest duty not done or

badly done leaves a lack or a blemish on the whole world's work. The great Arabian poet said: "Are you an artisan, a mason, a house-builder? Are you helping in building a house? Do it in the consciousness that your Beloved will occupy the house some day. Are you a weaver working on the loom? Weave your cloth in the consciousness that your Beloved will wear it some day!" There you have the secret of true work – work which will never be drudgery but always a source of joy.

Suggestion No. 7:

Be a master, not a slave. Be a master over circumstances, passion, desires and animal appetites. Therefore, learn self-control. Develop self-discipline. The man who is a slave to his desires and appetites soon finds that life becomes a burden. Do not allow yourself to be ruled or defeated by those things of which you should always be a master.

Suggestion No. 8:

Let go, let go, let God! If you are frustrated, disappointed, hurt, unhappy, if you find that, in spite of putting forth your best efforts, you have failed, then let me say this to you: - Let go, let go, let God! Let go of everything. Let God take charge of all your affairs! If only you can do this, you will find miracles happening in your daily life.

Begin right now to repeat the words: "Let go, let go, let God! As you continue to repeat this mystic formula, either silently or audibly, it will open the way for the flow of divine power, and you will be blessed.

Do you find yourself in a difficult situation? Are you passing through a period of storm? Are you in financial trouble, almost on the verge of bankruptcy? Are you filled with apprehensions in regard to some situation? Then let go, let go, let God! You will not be disappointed. You will find frustrations and fears dissolving. You will find tension and unhappiness vanishing. You will see limitations washed away and new opportunities open. God will work through you to bring your highest good into visible expression in your life. Letting go permits divine ideas to flow, divine light to shine, divine power to work, divine order and rightness to bless your mind, body and affairs.

6
TAKE SERIOUS THINGS LIGHTLY AND LIGHT THINGS SERIOUSLY!

Have you heard the beautiful song which beings:

> Little drops of water, little grains of sand
> Make the mighty ocean and the pleasant land!

It is the little things of life that count! But alas, in our mad rush for bigger and greater things, we ignore those little things that make life truly meaningful. Look at the huge banyan tree which spreads its leafy green branches so wide that dozens of people can rest comfortably under its shade. Do you realize that it has come out of a tiny seed!

Let us take care of the little things of life – and it is out of these little habits that our life is shaped.

There is an amusing story told to us about a king who built a magnificent temple of Lord Shiva. On the day of the consecration, he had arranged for a grand ritual of worship. So he ordered every citizen in the kingdom to bring one jug of milk and pour it into the temple's tank. This was to be done on the previous night so that the worship could start early in the morning.

Now, the citizens of the kingdom said to themselves, "Everyone is bringing one jug of milk. Who would know the difference if I took a jug of water instead? A little water would hardly make a difference in a tank full of milk!"

And so, under cover of darkness, everyone brought a jug of water and poured it into the tank, confident that no one would notice anything amiss. The next morning, it was discovered that the tank was filled with water. Not a single person had thought it his duty to offer a little milk for the Lord's special *puja*!

Everyone matters! Every little bit counts! I am sure you have all heard of the conundrum given below:

Something important had to be done urgently. Everybody thought somebody else will do it. So nobody did it. Anybody could have done it – but it was not done because nobody thought of doing it themselves!

Little things matter – and very often, so do little people! Do you know the height of Napoleon Bonaparte? He was barely 5'1"! As for Julius Caesar, he was just one inch taller, at 5'2". Arrogant Britishers described Mahatma Gandhi, as "that short, toothless person", "the half-naked fakir". This short, toothless, half naked fakir shook the mighty British Empire to its very roots.

Take light things seriously! Small things, small tasks are as important as the 'great' things of life. A perfectionist is one who pays as much attention to small details as to great tasks. Such a person peels an orange with as much care as he implements an important project. This is also the teaching of karma yoga which does not distinguish between 'low' and 'high' work in the execution of one's duty.

Take serious things lightly! Do not raise a storm in a teacup over trifling issues. It is only our inflated egos that lead us on to take offence over every trifling issue. Sometime ago, I read of a Union minister who decided to take a flight to his destination. As this was done at the eleventh hour, the minister could not be accommodated in the First Class which was already filled with passengers who had paid the full fare. The minister, who was getting a free ride, kept the flight waiting. When he saw that there was no vacancy in the First Class, he began to throw tantrums, and even threatened the flight crew with violent threats of dismissal. In his egotistical arrogance, he imagined that he could bully anyone and everyone into doing what he wanted. He thought too highly of himself – how could *he*, a minister, travel in the economy class with lesser mortals?

As it happened, there was a journalist on the same flight who recorded all that was happening. Then the event was reported in the media the next day, the minister's action was loudly condemned by everyone, and he was eventually forced to apologize for his disgraceful conduct.

Alas, many of us develop inflated egos and actually begin to believe that the world functions only because of us. But this is far from truth. None of us is indispensable. When you eliminate the ego, you will grow in the realization that all of us are equal in the eyes of God. Truly great men grow in humility as they evolve in stature. On the other hand, men who flaunt their wealth, power and possessions only reveal their immaturity.

Take light things seriously! Do everything in the spirit of offering to the Lord. It does not matter how lowly your station may be; it does not matter how humble the task you perform. It was Martin Luther King who said:

> If a man is called to be a street sweeper, he should sweep streets even as Michelangelo painted, or Beethoven played music, or Shakespeare wrote poetry. He should sweep streets so well that the hosts of heaven and earth will pause to say, "Here lived a great sweeper who did his job well."

Unfortunately, many of us are prone to equate "greatness" with fame, fortune and power. However, true perfection consists in the way we attend to life's little details. Therefore, we must concentrate on the task before us, the task at hand.

There was a spiritual seeker – a *jignasu* – who was told about a holy man, a sage who lived on a lonely, remote mountaintop. It was believed that this wise man had an answer for every question – the solution to every problem. Merely by spending a few minutes in his presence, one's life would be changed forever.

Naturally, the seeker was anxious to meet such an evolved soul. "If only I could just see him", he said to himself, "I would count myself blessed! If only I could share a few seconds with him, I would feel truly enlightened!"

He decided to set out in search of the sage's abode. For days together, he walked across hills, rivers, valleys and streams to locate the mountain where the great guru lived. After a tough and exhausting climb he finally arrived at the sage's front door.

Trembling with intense emotional excitement, he knocked at the door. It was opened by a lowly man in poor clothes whom he took to be a servant. The servant greeted him and led him through the house. They passed through several corridors and rooms, and the servant kept on talking as they walked. However, the seeker's mind was so fixed on the experience ahead of him, that he hardly paid any attention to what the man was saying. The servant glanced at him as he talked and, finally, they both arrived at a locked door. It led on to the backyard. Wordlessly, the servant indicated that the visitor should leave the house.

"But I've come all the way to meet the guru," the seeker protested. "I must have at least a few minutes with him!"

'You just did," answered the sage as he let the man out and shut the door firmly.

We are so preoccupied with 'big' issues, we have no time to spare for the *here* and the *now*. Our answers, the solutions to our problems are not always to be found on a mountaintop; they may be staring you in the face right where you are!

Some people alas, become permanent, professional 'seekers'. They are reading books, pondering deep questions, attending seminars and conferences on philosophy and spirituality and engaging in a lifelong quest. They forget that God can speak to them through the ordinary people they meet, through the grass, the flowers, the sun, the moon and the stars. They fail to realize that His ways are indeed mysterious, and that He can express Himself through the touch of a friend or the smile of a loved one or the shining eyes of a child.

Your *mukti*, your liberation, your salvation does not necessarily come from the hands of a powerful, impressive, authoritative figure. It can come to you through humble people whom you meet on the by-ways of life.

Take serious things lightly! Whenever the great inventor, Thomas Alva Edison felt lost and helpless and found it impossible to proceed with a difficult experiment, he would adopt a unique way out of the stressful situation. He would go to sleep on a couch holding tightly on to a rock in his hand. As he dozed, he would dip into his subconscious mind, where he knew the answer to his problems would be found. As he slipped into sleep, his hold on the rock would be loosened, and it would fall down with a thud. The noise would awaken Edison and he would spring up, awake and alert – the solution to his problem now available to him. He would quickly write it down and proceed with his interrupted experiment.

The noise, shout and shows of the world often distract us from the inner spirit, with its vast and deep store of wisdom. This inner genius can be tapped through deep relaxation. A good night's sleep, or a relaxing, short nap will clear the cobwebs of your mind, and allow your inner wisdom to shine forth.

We often dismiss the 'little' people and events of our lives.

We take our friends and family members for granted. By doing so, we simply overlook their special gifts and insights. It has been said that every person who walks the earth is a God in disguise. We celebrate a few great souls and extol them as 'leaders' – but what we must do is lift our vision and find the highest in those around us.

People seek fame and fortune in the world outside – as they believe that if they become rich and famous, they will also be happy and contended. They have got themselves slightly mixed up: if they do what makes them truly happy, appreciation and contentment will naturally follow.

After his life-changing experience in Walden, the American thinker and philosopher Thoreau went to visit his friend and fellow-intellectual, Emerson. He told Emerson all about his experience, living in the woods.

"What would you say is the most important lesson you learnt at Walden?' Emerson enquired of him.

Thoreau answered emphatically, "Simplify, simplify, simplify!"

Emerson smiled and responded, "I think one "simplify' would have done quite well!"

In a beautiful book called *Wisdom of the Heart*, best selling author Alan Cohen tells us: "the lighter we get, the higher we soar…we gain freedom in releasing possessions …and being able to appreciate the simple things of life…we recognize that simplicity is the flower that brings the intellect to its knees and recognizes the greatest riches of all."

Destiny and Responsibility

Take care of your fancies and imaginings.
They have magnetic power.
What you imagine today, determines what
your future will be.

J. P. Vaswani

1

THE CHANGING FORTUNES
OF LIFE

Our *rishis* and sages have repeatedly emphasized one fact: every incident, every accident that happens to us, happens because we deserve it. Good and bad fortune are not handed to us on a platter; we have earned them through our own actions. Every action we perform, every incident that befalls us, is a reaction to our past actions. But when misfortune strikes, we fail to realize this.

When they are faced with unpleasant or negative experiences, people react stereo typically: 'Why me? Why did it have to be like this?' These are the laments we hear at such times. The attitude of the sufferers is that they are innocent victims while someone else is the culprit, responsible for inflicting them with undeserved pain.

While we can sympathize with this attitude, we must realize that this will deprive us of the opportunity to reflect, introspect and recognize our own responsibility for our actions. In fact, by blaming others for our ills, we are only worsening the situation, or giving rise to new problems.

When we face whatever happens to us in a spirit of acceptance, we ward off very many negative feelings such as hatred, envy, malice and resentment. We rise above a sense of personal injustice and grow in the secure sense of Divine

Universal Justice. In such a spirit and such a mood, despair and misery are kept out, and we are not overwhelmed by what happens to us.

The story is the same wherever I go. People say to me: we have been honest and hardworking; we have not hurt or exploited anyone: we have done as much good as we could; and yet we have had to suffer. What could be the reason for this? Could it be that God is not really fair?

If you look upon life as a journey, as many great writers have done, then you will know that this journey takes us at times through pleasant green meadows and lush river valleys; but at other times, this journey takes us through dry, arid deserts and dark, mysterious woods. Every one of us knows this; everyone of us has experienced this in his or her own life. There are times when we feel on top of the world; there are times when we feel very depressed and despondent. When times are good, we are happy, we rejoice and offer gratitude to the Lord. But when things go wrong, we lose our equilibrium. We begin to question the justice of the Universe. It is at such moments that this question rises in the heart within – Is God fair? Is God really fair?

There is no question of any injustice in God's dispensation. I say again and again: God is too loving to punish, too wise to make a mistake. His dispensation of justice is simple and straightforward. He has no policeman to catch wrong doers; no courts to conduct endless trials; no judges to pronounce harsh sentences on those who are found guilty. God's dispensation is simple. Each one of us has been given a field of life. We are free to sow whatever we want in this field, which is our *karma-kshetra*. Only one condition binds us; we must reap what we sow. We must eat the fruits of our own harvest.

We are sowing seeds every day, every hour, every moment in the field of life. Every thought I think, every word I utter,

every deed I perform, every emotion, every wish that awakens within me – these are all seeds that I am sowing in the field of my life. In the course of time, these seeds will germinate and bear fruit. Bitter or sweet they may be – but I shall have to eat them. No one else can eat them for me. Where then is the question of God being unfair or unjust to me?

Life gives us many compensations and rewards – many more compensations and rewards than punishments and defeats. Life is a series of experiences. When we are passing through a difficult period, when we are confronted by experiences of misery and misfortune, adversity, illness, death, defeat and depression, we lament, we complain of god's injustice, we begin to ask, "Why is this happening to me?" But on the other hand, when we are passing through a happy phase, when we are blessed with special favours from God, it does not occur to any of us to tell God, "Why have you given me such happiness? I don't deserve it!"

There are numerous occasions in life when people get things that they never expected, or things that they have longed for all their life. After a long and frustrating wait, childless couples are blessed with offspring. Someone in dire need of money hits a jackpot. Another gets a long-awaited promotion. None of them ever think of telling God, "Why have you done this to me?" They simply assume that they have every right to the happiness that has come their way; they take it all for granted.

To people who come to me with bitter complaints against life, I pass on two sheets of paper. On one sheet I ask them to write all the cruel, the unfair, the unjust, the tyrannical, the dishonest and crooked things that they have done. On the other one, I ask them to write down all the good, the noble, the unselfish deeds that they have done in their lifetime. This is an exercise I recommend to you also, for it can be a real eye-opener for you.

When you have prepared these two lists, you will find that one list is much longer than the other. They do not balance each other. When you go through the lists, you will surely fold your hands in prayer before God and tell Him "God, be merciful to me, please forgive me, for all the wrong deeds I have done!"

This is the case with most people: their bad actions will by far outweigh the few good deeds they may have done. With such certain knowledge of our own balance-sheet of right and wrong, how can anyone of us claim that God has been unfair, unjust to us?

Finally, we must note that whenever suffering comes to us, God always gives us the strength and wisdom to bear it. For those are just two sides of the same coin – sorrow and wisdom, suffering and endurance. Look at the coin – on one side is suffering; on the other side is the wisdom and the strength to bear that suffering. Never, ever, does God send suffering to us, unaccompanied by the strength and wisdom to cope with it. That is why we continue to live, that is how mankind has survived personal and public calamities and still continues to flourish. The very fact that we are alive and breathing, is a testimony to this great truth – that we invariably conquer suffering with God-given strength and wisdom.

There was a man, who lost his only son in a war. He said to his friend, "when a man faces a loss such as this, there are only three ways out. The first is drink, the second is despair, the third is God. By God's grace, I have chosen the third option: Blessed Be His Name!"

2

THE LAW OF KARMA

What is karma? The law of karma has been described as the law of causation, the foundation on which this universe evolves. It is a universal law, an all-inclusive law which operates on the lives of all of us. It affects all aspects of our existence – spiritual, psychic, physical; it influences our thoughts, intentions, motives and action. It embraces our past, present and future, linked in a continuous cause-effect relation. The impact of this law is inescapable and inexorable. Its effect, reaction and response are absolutely impartial. We could say that it is the law of karma that upholds dharma, and maintains justice, equity, order and balance in the universe. The law of karma operates on individuals, as well as groups, communities, races and nations.

Any action, thought or feeling generated by an individual, brings with it certain indelible impressions, which are stored in the mind as *samskaras*. Every act, thought or feeling leaves behind a trace, which has the power to bring joy or sorrow. These traces, or karmic residue, can bring about consequences on three different levels:

1. The type of next birth – bird, animal, plant or human
2. Life span – long-lived or short-lived
3. Life experiences – pleasurable or painful

Karmic actions lead to results that may affect us in this

birth, or in lives to come. Thus, karma is closely linked with the concept of rebirth. This leads us to the next question. What happens to us in the interim between death and rebirth? Are all souls condemned to be born again and again – caught in the cycle of birth, death and rebirth?

According to Vedanta wisdom, there are four possibilities open to the soul after death:

1. For one who has attained enlightenment during this life, there is total liberation from the cycle of birth and death. Such a one attains *sadyah mukti* or instantaneous liberation and is not born again.

2. For one who has not attained liberation, but has achieved purity of mind and devotion to Brahman, there is a force which pushes the soul beyond the pull of this world and towards liberation. This is *krama mukti* – gradual or sequential liberation. In this process, the soul is led along a path of light and so attains an increasing expansion in consciousness until liberation is attained.

3. For one who has tried to live a virtuous life, but is not ready for liberation, there is a finite period of existence on the astral plane, where the astral body experiences pleasurable conditions. This is known as *swarga*. It is not liberation, but a relative experience of pleasure. This finite period is brought to an end when the soul's good karma is exhausted, and the soul is re-born into a new life.

4. For one who has accumulated no good karma at all, there is the painful fourth alternative – a period of intense suffering. But this period also comes to a close when the sinful karma is exhausted, and the soul is re-born in a new embodiment.

Thus, in the first two cases, liberation is attained. In

the third and the fourth, the soul must return to earth for the sake of its further evolution – after a period of either heavenly pleasure or hellish suffering. In these cases, karma will determine its next embodiment. For there are residues, remnants of karma that are not exhausted in the life-after-death state, be it heaven or hell. It is this residue or remnant that influences one's rebirth and life experiences. In other words, none of us is born into this world with what is called a clean-slate. Even what we consider to be hereditary traits are in reality determined by the karma of previous lives.

To sum up: our life now is the product of the karma that we have accumulated in previous births; simultaneously, this present life is also the seed of the future of our soul. We carry our past karmas with us; and this burden may have to borne by us even as we journey from life to life. The good and bad karma that we accumulate are entered in the credit and debit column of the account of our life. The balance is carried forward from one life into the next. This credit and debit is what we commonly refer to as *punya* and *paap*.

The law of karma is neither fatalistic nor punitive; nor is man a hapless, helpless victim in its bond. God has blessed each one of us with reason, intellect and discrimination, as well as the sovereign free will. Even when our past karma inclines us towards evil, we can consciously tune our inclination towards detachment and ego-free action, thus lightening the karmic load.

The law of karma is also the law of effort and destiny; the effort of yesterday is the destiny of today. The effort of today will be the destiny of tomorrow. Every effort that I am putting forth today is going to be my destiny tomorrow – may be, in a future life. The efforts that I have put in during my earlier life, have become my destiny today.

Sadhu Vaswani referred to the law of karma as the law of

the seed. He said to us, "Go and learn the law of the seed from any farmer, any peasant you meet. Any farmer will tell you that you will only reap what you sow. If you sow apples, you will reap apples. If you sow mangoes, you will reap mangoes. If you sow thorns, you will reap thorns."

The law of the seed, like the law of cause and effect, is universally applicable. You cannot get a reprieve from the law of karma. You can save yourself, however, by improving your karma. The seed you sow today shall grow into a tree and bear fruit; eat it you must, whether the fruit be bitter or sweet. We will have to face the consequences of our own actions. Nothing, no one, can save us from the law of karma. So powerful is the law that even Sri Rama could not save his father, King Dasharatha, from the consequences of his karma!

When Dashratha was a young bachelor prince, he once went into the forest, on a hunting expedition. At that time, the young hermit Shravan Kumar was also passing through the forest. He carried his old, blind parents with him, in two baskets that were slung across his shoulders. The old people were thirsty; so he put them down in the shade of a tree and went to fetch water. As he was filling his pitcher with water at a pond, he was hit by an arrow and fatally wounded. It was Dasharatha who had shot the arrow at him, for he had imagined that it was a deer which had come to drink water.

As Shravan Kumar lay in the agony of approaching death, Dasharatha realized that it was a yogi whom he had wounded. He was horrified. He rushed to the side of the dying man; he shed tears of bitter repentance.

"Oh prince, I don't have long to live", gasped Shravan Kumar. "I request you take this water to my aged, blind parents, for they both wait for me in thirst." So saying, the yogi passed away.

When Dasharatha conveyed the sad news of their son's

death to them, the helpless, blind parents could not contain their grief. In a fit of rage and sorrow, they cursed him. They said, "The day will come when what you have done to us will be done to you. Unable to sustain the loss of our son, we shall give up our lives today. May the fruit of your action rest on you! You too shall die of a broken heart, all alone! You too shall feel the loneliness of grief, as we do today. You will die because of separation from your dearly loved son!"

And so it came to pass, many years later, that when Dasharatha decided to crown Rama as the *yuvraj* that Kaikeyi, his second wife, took great offence. As a result of this Dasharatha had to banish Rama from the kingdom for fourteen years.

The law of karma is not punitive: it does not wreak vengeance. It is the fine art by which we may eventually transcend the cycle of birth and death. It works to put us on the path to perfection. In our ignorance and immaturity we may regard it as a form of punishment; but like a kind and caring teacher, God knows that these experiences are vital to our spiritual growth.

The doctrine of karma is essentially one of hope and encouragement. It is the best motivation we can have for right thinking, right action and right living. If only we understood this law in its fullness, our lives would be beautiful indeed! We would learn the virtues of peace and contentment. We would bear the burdens of life with patience and acceptance. People would rejoice even in suffering.

A recognition and full awareness of the law of karma can help us to face life with a positive outlook. It can evolve in us the spirit of willing acceptance, and thus help us evolve as masters, rather than as slaves of circumstances. Above all, we can take control of our own actions and thereby shape our own future positively.

Karma is a uniquely Hindu concept. But its basic tenets are reflected in many religions. Thus, the Bible tells us, "As you sow, so you reap." And further, "God will render to every man according to his deeds." Judaism says, "He who is liberal will be enriched, he who waters will himself be watered." I always say that people who hurt and kill in the name of religion, are killing their own brethren, for the surest way to reincarnate in a particular race or religion, is to hate that particular religion. It has truly been said that religious hatred and intolerance will become like the express train that will carry you into the religion you hate!

Karma is an opportunity to learn; karma is an opportunity to evolve spiritually; karma is an opportunity to repay all outstanding debts, so that we may be free to move onward, Godward! When we begin to understand the concept of karma we will never ever blame God for anything that happens to us. We will realize that we are responsible for all that happens to us. Rich or poor, saint or sinner, miser or philanthropist, learned or illiterate – as you sow, so shall you reap. This is the universal law that applies to individuals, to whole communities, societies, nations and races.

3

TYPES OF KARMA

In order to understand the balance of cosmic justice, it is necessary for us to grasp three different aspect of karma.

1. The first type of karma is *kriyaman* or *agami karma*. This is the karma of action and instant reaction. For example, you are thirsty and you drink water. Drinking water is an effort, an action. It produces an effect immediately – your thirst is quenched. The reaction cancels out the action and the karma is settled, on the spot; there is no residue to be carried over. Such an action has no effect on your future actions.

2. The second is *sanchita karma*, the sum total and store of all our actions, good and bad in the sequence of innumerable lives that we have lived. All of this is recorded and preserved.

3. The third type of karma is that part of our karma which matures, comes to fruition in one particular birth. This is *prarabdha karma*, and it is this karma which is the basis of our present birth, our present embodiment. Those of us who have been given the gift of human birth, we may be sure that this is the result of very good karma. Thus *prarabdha karma* on which our present existence is based, is often referred to as fate, destiny or luck, in popular language.

Sanchita karma, the second kind of karma mentioned above, is the karma that we have accumulated through numerous lives. All the actions we have performed – physical, mental, vocal – contribute to create this storehouse of karma. However, all this karma does not fructify, does not bear fruit at once. Only a small part of it fructifies in any one birth or embodiment. The rest of it remains accumulated – awaiting its fructification.

Let me give you a simple example. You appear for an examination: you do not get the result immediately. You have to wait for two or three months. In some cases, you may have to wait up to six months before your results are declared.

Our *sanchita karma* keeps on growing; in fact, it grows from birth to birth; it has been accumulating on a spiritual record through innumerable lives from time immemorial. The load of sanchita karma which each one of us carries is tremendous – indeed, a heavy load! All those karmas which do not produce their effect immediately are held in deposit – they are added to our accounts of karma.

Sanchita karma is karma that waits for an opportunity. It emphasizes the law that you cannot get away from anything. Let us suppose that there is a person who has borrowed one lakh rupees from you, and is unable to give it back to you; you go to a court of law and you get a decree against him. The bailiff goes to execute the decree, but finds that the man is bankrupt – he has no money to pay you. In such a case, the decree is not cancelled; it is kept pending. As soon as this man earns money, the decree will be executed against him.

Let us imagine, however, that this man dies before your loan has been repaid. The whole world would say, "He's been let off the hook," or, "He got away with it after all!" Well, he may have been let off from the point of view of the world: for indeed, our worldly courts can do nothing further with him – but his karma will not let him get away with it. The money that he owed to you, the money that he failed to repay, becomes part of his *sanchita karma*. In some future birth or births, he will have to repay this amount to you in the form of money or service. He may even be born as a bullock or an ox on your farm, so that he may pay off his debt through labour. The law of karma, as I said, is emphatic on this point. You cannot get away with anything!

In the story of the Mahabharata, King Dritarashtra demanded to know of Lord Krishna why God had afflicted him with blindness. With his yogic power, he could look back over one hundred previous births of his, and he could see that he had performed no such bad karma which would result in blindness. Then it was that Lord Krishna helped him go back even further; and he saw that several births earlier, he had blinded a swan and killed all its hundred signets. As a result, he was now born blind, and lost his hundred sons, the Kauravas, in the great war of the Mahabharata.

Ever since we first take human birth, action and reaction go on, and our karma accumulates. Some people perform negative actions, actions of adharma, yet they do not seem to reap the fruits of their bad actions. However, their bad karma lies latent, waiting to bear fruit. Similarly, the good karma of people who have performed virtuous actions may also be lying latent. One day, in some future birth, they will surely bring their reward.

Prarabdha karma, the third kind of karma listed above, is a part, or a fragment of *sanchita karma* which has fructified in this birth. Our sanchita karma accumulated over hundreds of births, is like a mountain; and in each life, we are adding to the store. Of this vast store, the *prarabdha* – the inevitable – is but a fragment. It is that portion of our karma assigned to us to be worked out in our present existence. It is also called ripe karma, for it is a debt which has become overdue, and must be paid back.

It is *prarabdha karma* which determines the family into which you are born. It determines the race, the nation in which you take birth. It also determines your sex, the type of body you will acquire, and so on. Remember this – your wealth is pre-determined. You may keep working all day, all night to get more money – but only that much money will come to you, which is permitted by *prarabdha*. Even if you get more, you will lose it through speculation, theft, etc.

For purposes of exhausting your *prarabdha karma* you need a physical body. It is only in this physical body that you can exhaust your prarabdha karma. And until it is exhausted, you will not be able to drop this body. You may be bed-ridden for years together, you may be afflicted with paralysis, or with some other crippling disease. You may be praying every day for your deliverance, and your near and dear ones may be praying for your deliverance, but you will not be delivered until you have paid off, exhausted through suffering or through enjoyment, as may be the case, your *prarabdha karma*. It is only when this *prarabdha karma* is exhausted that your physical body will drop down, and you will get a period of freedom, until you wear another physical body – to work out more karma that may have fructified in the meanwhile.

In the western countries, they talk of 'mercy killing' (surely a contradiction in terms!) to end the life of patients suffering from incurable and terminal diseases. Oh, it would be an act of kindness to release them from the agony that life has become – so we think! We could not be farther from the truth! For our present life – our condition, our circumstances, even our longevity, are all determined by *prarabdha karma*. Until this is exhausted, we cannot drop our physical bodies, however much we may long for release from the burden that life may have become. Indeed, our life will be prolonged – in some cases inexplicably; in some cases miraculously; in some cases against our own will – until every bit of our *prarabdha* is exhausted.

In total contrast to this, we also come across tragic deaths of the very young, including babies, small children and newly married couples. We grieve over such 'untimely' deaths – for they seemed to have a lifetime before them, and they have departed from this earth before they have experienced all that life had to offer to them. A tragic accident, a natural disaster, a sudden illness snatches them away, and we are not able to reconcile to their loss. Why? Why? We ask ourselves in bewilderment.

The answer is simple. Their fructified karma has been exhausted. The purpose for which they had to assume their physical body in this lifetime has been completed. Back their souls must return, to reap the rewards of this lifetime.

When I hear about the feuds between Hindus and Muslims, I am sometimes amused to think that some of these people who are fighting for Hinduism today, may actually have been Muslims in their previous birth! Equally, in a future birth, they may be reborn as Muslims! All these quarrels and feuds are meaningless – for your race and religion are also determined by your *prarabdha karma*. In any particular birth, while I am exhausting my prarabdha karma, I am simultaneously creating new karma. I may exhaust in this birth, one hundred thousand *prarabdha karmas*, but in the process, I create millions of other karmas, and these are added to my store of *sanchita karma*, and thus it goes on....

Thus 'destiny' is not something imposed on you from outside – you have built your own destiny through the efforts of yesterday. Yesterday's effort is today's destiny. Equally, today's effort is going to be tomorrow's destiny. Thus it is you yourself who are responsible for what is happening to you.

4

TAKE CARE OF YOUR SANGA

If you wish to evolve spiritually, if you wish to sow good karma, take care of your *sanga* – the people with whom you associate. If your company is right and good, your actions will also be right and good. Bad company will lead you to evil; good company will lead you on the path of virtue. In the stormy ocean that is *sansar sagar* (the sea of earthly life), sage Vashista tell us, *satsang* is like a boat that can carry us safely across to the other shore. It not only keeps you afloat in safety, but also transports you across to the other shore.

The value of *satsang* cannot be underestimated. Therefore does sage Vashista describe it as the personification of one of the gatekeepers of the heaven world:

"If you wish to enter the palace (i.e. attain liberation)," the sage tells Sri Rama, "you must make friends with the gatekeeper."

Narada, the sage whose life was devoted to his Lord Narayana, was on one of his pilgrimages. One night, he received the hospitality of a poor, childless couple, who served him with deep love and piety. In the morning, when Narada was about to depart, the householder humbly begged him, "You are beloved of Lord Vishnu. O please tell Him to bless us with a child."

Narada was so moved by the request that he made a

beeline to Vaikunth, where he met Lord Vishnu. "Dear Lord, be merciful to this humble devotee of yours. Bless that man with a child, " implored the sage.

"I am sorry," said the Lord. "It is not in the destiny of that man to have a child."

Narada went on his way, disappointed.

Five years later, happening to pass the same way, he was once again received by the hospitable couple. To his amazement, he saw not one, but two children playing at the door of the hut.

"Whose children are these?" he asked in disbelief.

"Ours", said the man. "Soon after you left us last time, our prayers were answered. My wife and I have been truly blessed."

Narada hastened to confront Lord. Vishnu. "How could you be so mistaken?" he shouted. "You said it was not in the destiny of that man to have children! Now he has two of them!"

The Lord laughed aloud. "That must be the doing of a saint," he said. "Surely you know Narada, association with a saint has the power to change destiny!"

Satsang can be translated to mean 'association with the good, the pure, the wise and the holy'. Regular association with such positive, healing forces can lead us on to discrimination (*viveka*) and hence to liberation (*mukti*).

Satsang works effectively to promote our spiritual well being. As we begin to relish the good counsel and the good thoughts that we imbibe in the *satsang,* we become more and more aware of the truth of human life. When our minds are illumined by the light of truth, we become equipped to face what Shakespeare described as "the heartaches and thousand natural shocks that flesh is heir to" – in other words, all the miseries that confront us in human life. *Satsang* is like the lamp that lights our way through the darkness of our life on earth.

A realized soul, an enlightened one, is like a centre of Light –' a living temple of the Lord towards which seekers travel, to find solace, comfort and good counsel. Since times immemorial, the devout of our land have sought out the abodes of the Lord, which have become centres of pilgrimage. The presence of a guru transforms the *satsang* into such a temple. Just as the temple is made holy by the living faith of the devout, so also is *satsang* made holy by the living presence of a *satguru*.

Indian culture and tradition have always emphasized the importance of the guru in the individual's search for liberation. This is because the intellect, on its own, cannot help us attain the truth. On the other hand, association with a saint will help us imbibe the truth we seek. From the presence of such a one, we assimilate goodness and virtue. When we have found such a noble soul, we need look no further.

Avidya (ignorance) and *kama* (desire) lead us on to bad karma. *Satsang* is the means by which we can conquer *avidya* and *kama*, thereby freeing our souls from the fetters of bad karma. All the negative aspects of our personality like envy, greed, hatred and despair are driven out of our system when we enter the *satsang*. Temptation ceases to trouble us. We are filled with the quality of *sattva*.

Satsang is one of the most potent means of energizing and elevating your subconscious mind, through powerful spiritual vibrations that emanate from the guru. This is reinforced by the faith and devotion of one's fellow aspirants who congregate there. Such good association can only do us good, by aiding our moral and spiritual growth.

Our great spiritual teachers liken the pull of *maya* to the gravitational force of the earth. The atman must ultimately free itself from this force in order to attain liberation. *Satsang* provides us with the strong spiritual upliftment that we need for this purpose. Just as rocket scientists work hard to increase the velocity of a spacecraft, so also the people who come together at the *satsang* cultivate spiritual understanding and divine guidance, to help each other progress and attain a higher plane.

We are constantly in touch with the lives and experiences of great souls and saintly personalities that are narrated in the *satsang*. This helps us realize that pain, suffering, defeat and adversity are not specific to our lives alone, and that virtue and goodness always triumph over the negative forces.

Little wonder then, that Sant Tulsidas tells us that if you were to place all earthly and heavenly joys on one side of the scale and the happiness of *satsang* on the other, the latter will outweigh the former. For human happiness is like cotton – bulky but insubstantial; while satsang is like a diamond – dense and strong, valuable and eternal.

WHAT IS SUFFERING?

Suffering is of two types:

1. There is the suffering we create for ourselves through violation of the laws of life – through impure thinking and wrong feelings; through wild imagination and unbalanced emotion, through harmful habits and unhealthy desires, and through a wrong use of our energies and powers to unworthy ends. Such suffering serves no useful purpose. Such suffering can, and should, be avoided by bringing our thoughts, will and imagination under control and by directing our energies to the fulfillment of life's true purpose on earth.

So many of us go out of our way to create unnecessary suffering for ourselves. The cause of most of our suffering is that we cry over split milk, we worry over things which have already happened and for which nothing can be done; we let this worry spoil our present: and we look with fear to an unknown future.

Fear of the future makes us imagine all sorts of horrible things. I know of a girl who, for many months, lived in mortal fear of a dreaded disease which she thought would soon overtake her. Her parents argued with her: eminent doctors examined her carefully and

pronounced the verdict that there was no chance of her being attached by that disease. All to no avail! Every moment of her life she lived in fear. She could not eat: she could not work: she lost all interest in life. Her suffering was terrible – until she met Beloved Dadaji (Shri T. L. Vaswani). He spoke to her lovingly. He let her open out her mind to him. He asked her to abandon all fear and, in its place, cultivate childlike trust in God, who is the loving Father-Mother of us all.

"In Thee I trust! To Thee I surrender myself!" When we grow in this attitude, we are freed from fear of the future and are saved much needless suffering. The future is not in our hands. We may not have a future at all. Or, when it actually comes, it may be so different from what we imagine it to be. The future has been concealed from us by a loving providence. Why probe into what God chooses to hide from us? To do so is to invite suffering. For, bitter is the fruit of man's wisdom. Let us trust without seeing. Let us live without trying to unveil that which has been veiled to our sight. Let us build our life in the words of Jesus which have a deeper practical significance than most of us may know: "Sufficient unto the day is the evil thereof."

2. The second type of suffering is that which comes to us from God. It is not the result of the violation of the laws of life. It comes to the best of men, to the noblest of souls. It came to Krishna and Christ, to Buddha and Zoraster, to Moses and Muhammad, to Nanak and Kabir, to Mansoor and Mira – to all lovers of God and Man.

This type of suffering does not come alone: it brings

the strength which endures, the comfort which lends sweetness to suffering. This is what distinguishes it from suffering of the first type. Unaccompanied, as it is, by the soothing touch of God, the suffering which man creates for himself becomes hard and unbearable: it breaks down his spirit and throws him into an abyss of grief and despair.

The suffering which comes to us from God is for our good: but we do not understand this until we have cast all thought of self aside. When the self is thrown off, then and only then do we behold the loving Hand of God in every circumstance and situation of life.

Everything that happens works for our good. The seeming cruelty and injustice of men, their selfishness and ruthless disregard of values we hold dear, are seen to be the results of God's infinite goodness and unfailing love.

Each one of us has so many lessons to learn: lessons which differ from individual to individual. The lessons meant for me are not the lessons meant for you. Therefore the trials God sends me are different from the trials He sends you. Trials must not be resisted. To resist is to make strong. Do not resist trials, but welcome them. Everything that we welcome is transformed. Suffering is transformed into love. This is the great mystery of life.

Physical pain, mental agony, spiritual anguish – nothing lasts for ever. Everything lasts for as long as it has its work to do. When it has completed its task, it falls away like the dead, dry leaves of autumn. Many are the problems and perplexities that a pilgrim has to face, as he treads the Path. He knows that every one of them is necessary. So he does not complain. But he accepts each difficulty as it comes, makes it a part of his life, is enriched by it and moves on one step nearer the goal.

There are periods when a pilgrim finds himself surrounded by utter darkness. At such times, he finds it difficult to welcome trials and temptations with enthusiasm: but in no case does he avoid them. Deep within him is the faith that though the situation be exasperating enough, if only he can be patient and trusting, God will come and lead him by the hand out of danger into security, out of defeat into victory, out of darkness into Light!

6
BELIEVE AND ACHIEVE

There was a man who had set out on a mission to go around the world on his bicycle. He came to meet my beloved Master, Sadhu Vaswani and said to him, "I have been on the road for over a year now. And during this year, there have been occasions when my spirits have fallen very low. I have felt discouraged and frustrated. Give me a few simple words that I can inscribe on my ring, so that whenever I feel depressed, I can look at the inscription and feel my spirits rising!"

Sadhu Vaswani thought for a brief while and then gave him these words: "Believe and achieve!"

These three words spell the secret of success: believe and achieve! Believe in yourself, believe in the work you have undertaken. Believe that you will succeed in your work. If you do not believe in yourself, how can you hope to succeed?

Believe and achieve! And in order to do this, faith is essential. It is a triple faith that men need today – faith in oneself, faith in the world around, which is not merely just but essentially good, and above all – faith in God. If you cultivate this triple faith, you are bound to succeed in whatever you do!

Believe in yourself – but which self? For you must remember, there are two selves within every man. There is a lower self, the ego self, the empiric self, the self with which we are only too familiar in our day-to-day existence. It is the self of passion and pride, of lust, hatred, greed, envy, jealousy, resentment, ill-will, selfishness and misery. Unfortunately we have identified ourselves with this self; we magnify it out of proportion in the course of our daily life. That is why in the world today, we have wars and violence, hatred and strife.

The lower self sits on the threshold of our consciousness, and easily catches us; it captures us, misleads us, leads us astray. And yet, it is just a tiny self. When you enter into the depths of meditation, you will realize that it is but a tiny speck of a speck of a speck of a speck. But because we have identified ourselves with it, we magnify it beyond all proportions and allow it to dominate our life.

But there is another self within each one of us – the larger self, the nobler self, the radiant self, the true self, the "self supreme" in the words of the Bhagavad Gita. In the measure in which you identify yourself with this higher self, in that measure success will come to you like an ever-flowing, ever-full river.

Some of you may have heard of the great Italian musician, Enrico Caruso. Of him Thomas Burke once said, "Enrico Caruso was not just a singer, he was a miracle!" Truly, Caruso was a miracle! It is said that when he sang with full-throated ease, the power of his voice, the vibrations of his music could actually shatter a glass to pieces. But Caruso was an utter failure when he began his career. When he gave his first performance, we are told that the audience was so disappointed that they actually took sticks in their hands to drive him off the stage.

Caruso was not the one to give up easily. He was found pacing up and down his room, fervently uttering the words which became the very mantra of his life. What were those words? "You little me, get out of me! You big me, get into me! You little me, get out of me! You big me, get into me!"

Throw out the ego self, the lower self, invite the big self, the self supreme to come and take charge of your life. Surely, you will believe and achieve!

On a cold winter's day, with the temperature below zero, an old pilgrim was making his way to a shrine in the Himalayas.

"My man" exclaimed a fellow traveler who passed by. "How will you ever get there in such a cold season?"

"My heart got there first," replied the man cheerfully. "It's easy for the rest of me to follow!"

Within each and every one of us is a tremendous potential to overcome obstacles and achieve success; to face difficulties and overcome them. There is just one thing we have to do to tap this vast potential, this tremendous power – we must believe in ourselves.

Walter Davis was a great athlete who believed and achieved. As a boy, he contracted infantile paralysis, and the doctors feared that he might not be able to walk again. His mother's loving care and attention put the boy back on his feet. As he began to walk slowly, he saw a boy doing high-jumps and thought to himself that it was something he would love to do. So he began practicing high jumps, until he became very good at it. But, his legs were still weak, and serious competition was out of the question for him. He, however, kept up his painstaking efforts to strengthen them. When he married, his wife understood his aspirations and said to him, "Walter, it is not enough to have power in your legs. You must have power in your mind!" She coined a new phrase for him: *the strength of belief*. This, she said would bring greater strength to his legs.

Strength of belief took Walter Davis to great heights. Eventually, it helped him create a world record. He cleared the bar at six feet eleven and five-eighths inches – propelled by his strength of belief. The boy they said might never walk again became the High Jump Champion of the world! Belief was his strength – he believed and achieved!

7

NEVER, NEVER, NEVER
GIVE UP!

Whenever you have a goal before you, whenever you have set out to accomplish something, you must never, never, never give up. If you are sure that you have chosen the right goal, if you are confident that it is the right thing to do, that it will not hurt or harm anyone – never, never, never give up!

Difficulties may arise, obstacles may impede your progress, you may fail again and again. But as I have said earlier, failures are not final. They are only the stepping stones to success. All the great ones of humanity who have achieved success in life are the ones who have never, never, never given up. Whenever you take up a work in hand, you must see it to the finish. That is the ultimate secret of success. Never, never, never give up!

Gautama Buddha, the enlightened One, attained his goal only through dedicated determination and unflinching perseverance. Many were the gurus he had sought; numerous were the paths he trod; punishing were the austerities he practiced. At the end of it all, he was reduced to an emaciated, weakened man, almost crippled by self-inflicted torture. And his goal – enlightenment – was nowhere in sight!

Gautama turned away from extreme austerity and penance. He took a little nourishment to revive his failing strength and sat down under the Bodhi tree. He was determined that he

184

would not leave it until he had attained enlightenment. His body could wither away, his skin might shrivel and fall, his bones might crumble to powder – but he would not give up until the desired goal was achieved!

How can success – even the greatest spiritual triumph – evade such dedication and determination?

You have no doubt heard the name of Webster – Daniel Webster who gave his name to the well-known dictionary. Do you know how long it took him to prepare the very first edition of the dictionary named after him? Thirty six years! For thirty six long years, he laboured, he toiled ceaselessly. He could have given up after five years, or ten years or fifteen years. But he did not give up.

It took Gibbon twenty-six years to write that memorable book, The Decline and Fall of the Roman Empire – twenty-six painstaking years! Gibbon did not give up his labour of love until it was accomplished.

Many are the discoveries made by scientists who never, never, never gave up, when defeat stared at them in their faces. Consider for a moment, the countless examples from history of people who never, never, never gave up! Henry Ford failed and went broke five times before he finally attained success. Beethoven was not defeated by deafness. He transcended his handicap to compose the most magnificent symphonies. Deaf, speechless and blind since early childhood, Helen Keller achieved the kind of greatness that few people have ever achieved.

The difference between the impossible and the possible, it is said, lies in a man's determination. Never, never, never gtive up!

A broken tired, defeated man went to see his Rabbi, seeking comfort and guidance in his deep despair.

"Help me, Rabbi!" he cried. "I'm so tired of failing. Nothing I try ever seems to work. What should I do?"

"I'll tell you what to do," said the Rabbi. "Go and look on page seven hundred and twenty of the *World Almanac*."

The man went to the library, located the book and turned to page seven hundred and twenty. He found a list of the batting averages, of the great baseball players of the world. At the top of the page was the name of Ty Cobb, the greatest slugger of all time. His average was three hundred and sixty seven.

Puzzled, the man went back to the Rabbi. "I don't understand," he said. "What am I supposed to learn from Ty Cobb's batting average?"

"He was the greatest of them all," said the Rabbi. "His average was three hundred and sixty seven which means – one out of every three times he stood at the plate, he got a hit. But two out of every three times, he *did not* get a hit. And he was the greatest."

Life is not a matter of simple victory. We fail, we fail and we fail, until finally, we succeed. There are always going to be discouraging times when we want to give up, and walk away from it all. But perseverance is that voice inside you, which says, "Never, never, never give up!"

Listen to this voice, if you wish to succeed!

From the Material to the Spiritual

Look at yon tree! It is bound to the earth,
yet it seeks the sky. And never has
it questioned why.

J. P. Vaswani

1
THE WORLD HAS
A MEANING

The world is not an illusion, but has a meaning. We are here to express Eternity. We have entered into the fields of space to express the Eternal in time. Each one of us is essentially of the Eternal. Deathless and immortal are we all, though we are clothed in bodies which must, one day, perish and die. The body is perishable; but that which dwells within the body is immortal. The body is a cage: it must, one day, drop. The bird that dwells within the cage will fly away.

The Rishis of the Upanishads emphasize this thought, again and again. And in a number of *slokas* in the *Gita* the same thought has been beautifully expressed:

> *O Arjuna!*
> *The atman is the Eternal in man:*
> *He is never born, and he never dies!*
> *He is in Eternity: he is for evermore!*
> *He does not die when the body dies!*
>
> *Even as a man casting away an old garment,*
> *Puts on one that is new,*
> *Even so the atman leaves his mortal body*
> *And enters one that is new.*

Weapons cannot cleave the atman:
And fires can never burn him!
Untouched is he by drenching waters:
Untouched is he by parching winds!

The *atman* is the Hidden Self in man. And turning away from the *atman*, man wanders, from unrest to unrest, in hot pursuit of shadow-shapes that come and go. Man's life on earth is an aimless wandering until he learns to look within himself and makes the greatest discovery of his life – the discovery of the *atman*.

He who would set out in search of the Hidden Self must do two things. He must 1) look within; and 2) make his life a *yagna*, an offering to the Eternal. His life must become "a sacrifice, charged with divine forces, for the highest service of humanity and all creatures – for all the children of the One Supreme." These two things make the life of man truly beautiful. These two things were conspicuous in the life of Sadhu Vaswani as they were in the lives of St. Francis and Mahatma Gandhi and Annie Besant. They all realized that "the world, though transient, is not a phantom, but has a meaning." And in diverse ways they showed what it was "to express the Eternal in time."

To express the Eternal in time one must eliminate desires. One must transform them into aspirations. As man learns more and more to transform desires into aspirations, he grows in the beauty of the "balanced life". The Gita says:

From the world of the senses
Ariseth heat and cold,
Pleasure and pain.
They come and they go:
Rise above them, O Arjuna!
The man whom these torment not,

189

Who is steadfast,
Balanced in pleasure and pain,-
He is fitted for life in Eternity!

Pleasure and pain control us. But the man who discovers the Hidden Self is not overwhelmed by pleasure and pain. He is free from the pairs of opposites. He has touched the mid-point, the neutral point, where dwelleth God. And out of him flows an endless, ceaseless stream of blessing. He continuously gives out blessing and benediction to all who cross the pathways of his life. He blesses all men he meets, all things he sees, all events and incidents which enter into his life. He blesses all men – good and bad, friends and foes, rich and poor. He blesses all situations, pleasant and unpleasant. He blesses strangers on the roadside, the sick in hospitals, the peasants working in fields and farms, the labourers toiling in factories. He blesses brother birds and animals and prays that they may live in peace. He blesses the very trees on the wayside. He blesses all creation. And, again and again, he breathes out a simple prayer: "May all be happy and full of bliss!"

Of such a state speaks the Buddha in words of penetrating beauty:

"We live happily, indeed, not hating those who hate us! Among men who hate us we dwell free from hatred!

"We live happily, indeed, free from ailments among the ailing! Among men who are ailing let us dwell free from ailments!

"We live happily, indeed, free from greed among the greedy! Among men who are greedy let us dwell free from greed!

"We live happily, indeed, though we call nothing our own! We shall be like the bright gods, feeding on happiness!

"Victory breeds hatred, for the conquered is unhappy. He who has given up both victory and defeat, he, the contented, is happy!"

An Iranian king once said to a scholar: "Give me a summing up of human life in a few simple words."

The scholar thought for a week, then met the king and said to him: "Sire, in these few, simple words is given us a summing up of the entire human life: He was born: he grew in years: he married: he begot children: he died!"

Is this all there is to human life? Those words describe the animal aspect of human existence: but man is more than an animal. It is true, men are born, and so are animals. Men grow in years, so do animals. Men marry. I am not sure if animals also marry, but I know of at least one instance in which an animal couple was brought together in wedlock. I received a wedding card from a wealthy man, inviting his friends to the marriage of his male dog to a female one belonging to another wealthy man. The marriage was to be solemnized in the crystal ball room of a five-star hotel. I cannot say if the couple was faithful to each other, but the marriage did take place.

Man begets children, so do animals. Man dies, and so do animals. Is man only an animal? Is this all there is to human life? Is there not a higher element in human life, which makes the human birth priceless? We must rise from the animal stage of existence to the human. Therefore, we must learn the lesson of self-control.

Life should not be a great effort, for in truth, life is the effortless way. Even as the river flows on, singing its songs to the moving winds and the patient trees, even as the river flows on without effort, even so must life be lived in the effortless way. Even as the sun shines without effort, sending forth its life-giving rays of warmth and light, even so must life be lived in the effortless way. Life is given us to live: and if we lived in the right way, living would be as simple as breathing. One meaning of the world, "life" is "breath". And life should be as natural, as easy, as uncomplicated as breathing.

Within every man is the hidden soul, the over-soul, which the *Gita* and the Upanishads refer to as the *atman*. It is the larger Self, the greater Self of man. The tragedy of most of us is that we are unaware of this Higher Self which is our True Self. We live within the confines of the finite self which is the self of cravings, desires and appetites. Little wonder, our lives are cribbed, cabined, confined. We live in a prison-house of our own creation. We have reduced ourselves to creatures of circumstances. We are swayed by every passing wind of impulse or emotion. We live unhappy lives.

Man, today, has become a searcher of space. He has set out on the outward journey: he is eager to visit the moon and the planets. He wishes to build colonies in space. When man learns to look inward, when he sets out in quest of himself, when he finds his True Self, the *atman*, he will know that he is not a creature of circumstances, swayed to and fro by the passing winds of events and incidents, but a master of life, a co-partner with God in the great Plan of Creation. United with the Will Divine, the *atman*, he will become a man of wisdom.

2
THE IMPORTANCE OF SILENCE

All physical, mental and intellectual effort uses up energy. To make good this loss, we require repose. Even as night follows day, rest and relaxation must follow stress and effort. Of course, restful sleep at night is vital for our well-being. But apart from this, I recommend strongly, the practice of silence during the day.

We live in a world where everyone talks far too much! We talk excessively in public and in private. As a wise man said, "Men seem to feel the need to cloak and excuse their imperfections and wrong deeds in a mass of prattle." We need to devote a few minutes each day to the healing, soothing, purifying influence of silence.

Silence is relaxation for the mind, even as rest is relaxation for the body. It should be our earnest effort, at least once a day, to escape from the stress, strain, tension and turmoil of life, and practice absolute silence. We can easily give up mindless activities like watching TV or gossiping with friends, to devote to the practice of silence.

Silence helps us commune with the inner Self, silence enables us to discipline our petty, calculating intellect. Silence takes us close to God. In silence, we can feel our prayers reach Him and in perfectly held silence we may even hear His answers to our prayer!

I call my habitual hours of silence, my "daily appointment with God." It is vital that we cultivate the healing habit of silence in this age of noise and ceaseless activity. In fact, the great need of modern man is silence. To help us to avoid stress and tension, the noted psychologist, Deborah Bright, recommends what she calls PQT – Personal Quiet Time – or twenty minutes, twice a day.

Even as particles of dust cling to our clothes, so too, particles of noise cling to our hearts. To clean our clothes, we wash them with soap and water. Even so, to cleanse our souls, we need to take a dip in the waters of silence every day!

Silence heals, silence soothes, silence comforts, silence purifies, silence revitalizes us. In this world of allurements and entanglements, the sharp arrows of desire, craving, animal appetite, of passion and pride, of ignorance, hatred and greed, wound our souls again and again. Our souls bear the scars of many wounds. Silence is the great healer that can heal these wounds.

We must remember that silence is two-fold. There is the outer silence; it is absence of noise, freedom from the shouts and tumults of daily life. And there is interior silence; it is freedom from the clamour of desires, the cessation of mental acrobatics, the stilling of the play of conflicting forces. It is the peace that passeth, surpasseth understanding. Not until we have reached this peace, can we hope to experience unbroken joy and harmony for which our distracted hearts, minds and souls cry out constantly.

The powerful effect of the spirit on the body is generally recognized today. As I have stressed repeatedly, the body cannot be healthy if the soul is sick. Therefore, we may conclude that if we wish to be healthy, we also have to be 'holy'.

Do not be alarmed by that world 'holy'. It does not really mean what you think – pious and devout to a fault. The word 'holy' comes from the anglo-saxon root "wholth" meaning the entire being. Spiritual harmony is absolutely vital to combat the physical disharmony that we call disease. Spiritual harmony is best cultivated by the practice of silence.

It is reported that neuro-surgeons are conducting advanced research into methods of alleviating pain with supersonics. These are said to be ultra-high frequency sound waves that are used to destroy pain pathways in our brain. I am sure that the practice of silence can set in motion spiritual high-frequency waves which will bring God's own healing power to destroy pain.

A doctor I know had to treat a woman patient suffering from a severe throat infection and chest congestion. He wrote out a simple prescription for her: *Complete and utter silence.*

'Did the prescription really work?" I asked him.

"Sure it did," he replied. "The patient was indeed suffering. Her symptoms were real, but I could not medicate her because I knew her affliction was not physical."

"Did she get better?" I persisted.

"In body, mind and spirit," answered my friend.

Dr. Albert Schweitzer said, "Each patient carries his own doctor inside him. We are at our best when we give that doctor a chance to work on the patient." God has given us all the power of healing ourselves. All we need to do is to allow this power to work and there is no better way to do this than the practice of silence.

When we shut out the harsh and grating noises of the world – the deafening sound of men, machines, automobiles, strife, arguments and clashes – our hearts and minds are quietened, and we listen to the divine harmony within us. It is of this divine harmony that Shakespeare writes:

Such harmony is in immortal souls;
But while this muddy vesture of decay doth grossly
Close it in,
We cannot hear it.

Beautiful and serene is the silence of the spirit! When we enter its realm, we experience peace, harmony and a sense of well-being. Our ego gives way to divine love. Our stress and tension melt away. In this condition, we can listen to our inner voice which can help us solve the most difficult problems of this life.

Have you seen a plant that has not been watered? Its leaves grow pale, its flowers wither, and it droops miserably. The moment you nourish the plant, the leaves regain their lost freshness and greenness. Gradually, the flowers recover their beauty and fragrance, and the plant is restored to life. What you have done is to water the roots, to work this miracle of recovery. Silence waters the very roots of your life. When you open the windows of your heart and soul to receive the silence of the spirit, you lift your consciousness to bathe in the waters of divine healing.

Hippocrates, the Father of Medicine, felt that the force responsible for healing the human body, was a life-force that resides within us. He called it by the Greek name, *pneuma* – from which we derive the words, *spirit* and *soul.*

The Roman physician Galen, also believed in the holistic healing of body, mind and soul. He is known to have said, "I bind the wound, God heals it." The healing, God-given force that resides within us, can be released for our benefit when we cultivate silence.

It seems to me that many people today are terrified of silence, afraid of being alone. I know several couples who do not like to spend a quiet evening at home by themselves.

They invite friends over, or go over to clubs or to restaurants so that they do not face solitude. I even know a few people in whose homes the TV is always switched on – even when no one is watching it! They tell me it is comforting to hear the sound from the TV!

Why are we afraid of solitude and silence? Possibly because we cannot bear to look deep within ourselves. This is why, many people say they don't have time for silence or meditation. But they will realize, when they go deep within themselves, that the Infinite is within – and we have nothing to fear!

3

THE MAGIC POWER OF PRAYER

There was a time when it was believed that dreamers, visionaries, preachers, pujaris, housewives all believed in prayer. Prayers, however, were not for the rational man, the man whose brain was developed. Today, my friends, a number of scientists are bearing testimony to the power of prayer. There is that great statistician, Bobson who says: "The greatest undeveloped resource of the world is faith and the greatest unused power is prayer." There is tremendous power in prayer, but we have not used it.

The great Nobel Laureate Alexis Carrel said on one occasion: "Prayer is the most powerful force that anyone can ever generate." It is more powerful than atomic energy for it is *atmic* energy. Prayer is *atmic* energy. It is the most powerful force that anyone can ever generate. Prayer is as real as terrestrial gravity. You know of gravitational force. If I hold this card in my hand and then let it go it falls to the ground. That is gravity. Carrel says that prayer is as real as terrestrial gravity. He says, "I have seen men, after all other therapies have failed. I have seen them come out of disease and melancholy by the serene effect of prayer."

Carrel was a doctor and he says that from his own personal experience he could say that when all other therapies had failed, people could still come out of disease by prayer. He goes further to say that "the world today stands on the edge of destruction because the people have forgotten to pray." He says that if only we started to pray the condition of the world would be different. We would be able to change, make the world new. There is so much power in prayer, but we have not used it. It is there before us. Ah! That is the question, why do we not pray! Whey do we not do so?

There is that great scientist, also a Noble Laureate, Pierre Curie, the husband of Marie Curie. At the turn of the century he gave a new direction, a new dimension to science. Scientists had believed that they had reached the end of knowledge, at the end of the 19th century. They were full of self-assurance. They said that there was nothing more left to be known. Once Pierre Curie was working in his laboratory bent over his microscope. A student happened to enter the laboratory and seeing Curie bent over thought that he was offering a prayer. So quietly he tiptoed out of the lab. He realized that when you are praying you don't wish to be seen and in any case you don't wish it to be know that you have been seen. So the student quietly walked out. Pierre Curie found him walking out and immediately called to him and asked him why he was leaving. When the student came forward he found that Curie was only stooping down, looking through a microscope. So he said to him, "Sir, when I entered the lab I thought that you were offering a prayer. So I wanted to leave you in your quiet, in your silence." And do you know what words Pierre Curie replied? He said: I am praying, I was praying, all my work is prayer."

Just imagine! These are the words of a scientist not those of a Rishi or a sage. Curie says "All science study and research is a prayer. It is a prayer that God will reveal his eternal secrets to us for God does have secrets which he reveals only when man searches reverently for them. God did not make all of his revelations in the past. He is continually revealing himself, his plans and his truths to those who will search for them."

So the question is why do we not pray? Many answers are given to this question. One of the most common is that we have so much work to do. There is so much of haste, hurry and worry in life that we can't find the time to pray. In our own language, the Sindhi language, we say that I am burdened with so much work that I can't find the time even to scratch my head, so from where will I find the time to pray. But remember, this is only an excuse. The truly busy man always has time for many other things. If you want a thing to be done, don't go to a lazy man. He will tell you I have no time, but if you go to a busy man, he will tell you I'll find time for you. Just try it. It is only the busy man who can do work.

This is a very common reason that people give for not praying. They say we are so busy. My friends, remember it is God who gives you 24 hours in a day and night cycle. What if he were to say, now your time is over! You would drop down. There are people who while talking have dropped down, while giving lectures, have dropped down. God gives us 24 hours in a day and we are not able to spare even five minutes of time to him, just to express our gratitude for what he has done.

There are people who will tell you, we would pray but we lack faith. That is an understandable answer. You do need to have a living faith in prayer to be able to pray, otherwise your prayers will be only mechanical. You need to have an experience, a confrontation with God. It is only then that you will realize the magic power of prayer. There are people who have that experience. And if you have one single experience of that type, I tell you, you will not cease to pray. Then your prayer will be unceasing.

There are people who tell me "we are so evil, we are so wicked, we are so afraid of approaching God. Again an understandable answer, but I will come to it in due course. But may I tell you what is the real reason for our not praying? We do not pray, because we don't feel the need to pray. Most people say, we have everything that we need, what shall we pray for? They say this because they do not live a true life, they only exist. We eat, we get up from our beds, we go to work, we come back, read the daily newspaper. That is our life. Is it any better than animal existence? Animals eat, we eat. Animals work, we work. Animals procreate, we procreate. Animals die, we die.

We don't pray, because we don't feel the need to pray. Our needs are so few. I sometimes wonder, we are satisfied with little things. A human being must not be satisfied with little things, he must aspire for the highest. It is only when adventure enters our life that we feel the need for prayer. The call to adventure, the need for prayer, both go together. We must want to do some great things in life, we must have high ideals, we must have great hopes, we must have wonderful expectations. It is only then that we feel the need for prayer.

There was a girl, who said to me, "Do you know I spend most of my time in prayer." She is a college student. I said, "that's wonderful. You are one of the exceptional girls who believes in prayer." I then asked: "What is the reason for your praying so much?" She said, "I have fallen in love with a young man and I have been praying that our respective parents permit us to marry." Now there was a need. She had that need and she said she went on praying, praying, praying. The real reason is that we do not feel the need for prayer. If only we felt the need, prayer would become a spontaneous thing, it would come automatically.

Once your prayers are answered, you acquire a living faith in prayers. You then believe that your prayers are going to be answered, you have only to ask. There are people who tell me, why should we ask? You say that God is a loving father. We have also been fathers, we don't want our children to ask for things. We just provide them with those things. Never has a child come to me and said, "Father give me my daily bread, give me my food. Why should I go to my father, the Divine Father and ask him for things? He knows my needs, he must fulfill them."

Yes, my friends, there are needs for which we don't need to ask, we give to our children what they need, we give them food, clothing and shelter. But there are other things which we do not provide until the boy asks. Say, for instance, a motor cycle, do you give that to a child before he asks for it? There are so many things that our children need to ask of us and it is only after they ask that we think, consider whether those things should be given or not. Asking is not a condition of God's giving. Asking is a condition of our ability, our willingness to receive it.

I remember there was a boy who was pushed by his father to enter medical college. He could not pass even the first examination. He tried five times, every time he told his father. "Father I am not meant for it, I never asked for it, you have simply pushed me into it!" Now asking is only a condition of our ability to receive, our willingness to receive what is asked for. Therefore we need to ask for many things in prayer.

There are four answers that God gives to our prayers. The first is when we ask for a thing, we pray to God and he says, "Yes, my child, I am going to give it to you." The second is no, my child I will not grant your prayer. The third is wait. The time is not yet ripe. The fourth is, you ask for this but there is something better that I want to give you. When the answer is in the affirmative we feel very happy, we praise God and we say what a loving God you are. That makes our faith in God stronger. It is the other three answers that test our faith.

Faith, true faith is something that never breaks. It is because we don't have faith, because we have faith only in our ego self that when something happens which our ego self is not able to understand or grasp, that we say our faith is broken.

When God says no, the man of faith believes that there is a meaning of mercy in this too. God does not wait to give me this. It is for my good. Suppose a child were to come and ask you for a match box or for poison or for a razor, would you pass it on to him? You would not, you would say, no my child I will not give this to you because this will harm you. So there are certain things that God in his Divine wisdom will never grant you because he will never make a mistake. He knows what is good for me and what is good for you. He will provide only that which is good for us, nothing else. For each one of us individually he has a plan and his plan is a perfect plan. If what I ask for subscribes to that plan he will grant it, not otherwise.

It was Jean Inglo who said, "I have lived long enough to be able to thank God for many of my prayers which he did not answer." Our wisdom is limited. God is all wisdom, God is all love. He is too loving to punish, he is too wise to make a mistake. Therefore whatever comes from him is for our good, for our highest good, for our ultimate good.

There is a prayer that is ascribed to Plate in which he says: "O Lord of Lords! Grand me the good even though I do not ask for it. Keep me away from evil even though I ask for it.! He means, I don't know what is good for me and what is bad for me. You know better. I may in my foolishness ask for something which is bad for me. Please don't give it to me and once again, in my foolishness, I may ask you to keep away something which is good for me. Please give it to me. This is a prayer that we all need to pray, again and again.

Now, how does one pray. There are people who say that we

want to pray but we do not know how to. So let us understand what prayer is. There is nothing complicated about prayer. Prayer is as simple as talking to a friend. Remember God is the friend of friends. He is our one constant unchanging friend. He has been our friend not only in this birth but in birth after birth. Other friends come and go but he is the one constant unchanging friend.

It is also important to remember that you don't have to go to a particular place to pray. You don't have to go necessarily to a temple or to a church. It is, no doubt, good to go to these places for they are charged with holy strong vibrations. They will do you good, but for prayer it is not necessary. You can pray right here in the midst of a crowd. And until you have learnt to pray in the midst of a crowd you have not yet learnt to pray truly. All you have to do is to close your eyes, shut out the world for a moment and talk to God. Start talking to him.

In the beginning it will be a one way talk. You will be talking and you will not hear His voice. A stage comes when you hear the voice of God, but in the beginning you will do the talking and you will not get the answer. You will not listen. You will not be able to listen to the answer, but remember, he is listening to you. He is hearing you. In the beginning you may not be able to see the face of your beloved, but remember he is watching you, he is seeing you. That is prayer. Right now you can pray. God! I have pain in my heal. Will you relieve me of it? Just do it. Begin with something. As I said, you must have that urge that desire, keen desire that eager urge. It must wake up. And God is available to you all the 24 hours of the day and night. In the middle of the night you wake up, it's a sleepless restless night. Talk to God, he is by your side, he is there ready to listen to you. Just open out your heart to him.

Therefore, as I very often say, you must establish some link of love and devotion with God or a Godman. It may be the link of a child to his father or that of a friend to a friend or that of a brother to a brother, but establish that link and go to him again and again. This is very important. You must go to God again and again in prayer. It was a Chinese philosopher who said: "You must visit the house of your friend often otherwise weeds may grow in the path and you may not be able to find the house." So you must go to God again and again. Prayer is something very simple. All other things you have to learn, but prayer has no technique. It is just like that, just going to God.

Your prayers are not complete until you have prayed everyday for at least one person who has mistreated you, at least someone who has spoken ill of you, at least someone who has cheated you, exploited you, harmed you, wronged you, spread a scandal against you, because until you do that your prayers don't have that power. You can pray that health be given to a dear one, you can pray for the safety of your children who are very far away from you.

There are people who think of God with form. In truth God is beyond form and formlessness, but there are some who think of Him with form. There are some who think of Him as a formless being. So it depends upon your temperament, your nature. But it is always easier for most of us to think of God with form. That facilitates concentration and, in due course, that concentration leads to absorption.

Concentration comes out of eager desire. Whenever there is that eagerness, concentration becomes automatic. Therefore, I said, so many of us do not pray because we have not yet realized the need for prayer. Our lives are humdrum and mundane.

Prayer is the swiftest and surest way to establish a link with God. It cleanses your thoughts, purifies your mind and elevates your consciousness. It enables you to talk to God directly – and much more effectively than you can to people. For you can be sure that God listens carefully to every word you say!

Opening your heart to God is the most effective form of prayer. I urge my friends never, ever to forget their "daily appointment with God" as I call it – a brief, simple prayer first thing when you get up, and a quiet, reflective prayer before you fall asleep at night. You may utter prayers from the scriptures; or use your own words when you pray. The language of the heart is the best for any prayer!

4

THE SPIRITUAL PATH

I often think the spiritual way is made up of three steps. The first is longing, yearning. The seed of longing is implanted in every heart, it sprouts at its own time. And once it sprouts it makes the heart restless. Often the person feels unhappy, miserable. Nothing can bring comfort to him. The wealth of the world, its honour and power are to him, as ashes and dust. He has seen through the vanity of worldly life. He now longs for God alone, and for someone who may show him the way to God. One mark of this longing is tears. His eyes are filled with tears. He weeps, again and again, and out of the anguish of his lonesome heart cries out. "Where are Thou, Beloved.? Hide not They Face from me! In separation from Thee, every day is as an age!"

He sets out in quest. This is the second step on the path. He is in search of his Guru. He little knows that the Guru is already in search of him and at the right time will appear to him. In our ancient scriptures it is written that "when the disciple is ready, the Guru appears."

Then the disciple takes the third step. When the Guru has appeared to him and accepted him as his disciple, he has but one thing to do. It is obedience. Implicit, unquestioning obedience is what is asked of every disciple. This obedience is not merely mechanical. If it is mechanical, it will reduce the

disciple to an automaton and will make him utterly unfit for the creative action to which he is called. True obedience is an act of the will.

The disciple surrenders his will to the will of his Master, the disciple's will is blended with that of his Master. So is the disciple released from the bondage of the ego, from the clutches of his carnal self, his lower self of pride and desires and appetites. The disciple is liberated and he enters into the life of freedom, the freedom which belongs to the sons of God. The disciple becomes a child of God. His travail is over; his journey is complete; he has reached the goal.

There are as many ways to realize God, says a Sufi mystic, as are the breaths of man. Let each one follow the way to which he feels drawn. Of these one is the "little way". The "little way" is the way of love. It is the way of humility and child-like faith. Love, humility and faith – the three are inter-related.

In love you become truly humble, you become nothing, nothing: you lose all sense of "I-ness. And out of your heart there comes forth but one cry – "Naham! Naham! Tuho! Tuho!" I am not! Thou alone art!"

The truly humble man tries to conceal himself: he does not seek the praise of men. He does his work in a quiet way, without show or ostentation, realizing full well that by himself he can achieve nothing. It was Swami Vivekananda who said: "With God you can cross over the seas. Without God you cannot go over the threshold!" All credit belongs to the Lord.

The man of true humility is a man of forgiveness. If someone has injured or hurt him, he forgives the offender even before forgiveness is asked.

The man of humility never thinks of avenging himself. He forgives the wrongs that have been done to him and prays for the wrong-doers, in the immortal words of Blessed Jesus: "Father! Forgive them, for they know not what they do!"

Out of humility grows the spirit of surrender. Knowing that I am nothing, I can do nothing, I naturally seek refuge at the Lotus-feet of the Lord, who is my all. He is Infinite Love: and He is Infinite Wisdom. His love takes care of us all, as a mother takes care of her children: and His unfailing wisdom guides us in the right way, the only way which leads to our highest good. All that we are required to do is to abandon ourselves completely to the Lord, accepting every situation and circumstance, as it arises, trusting that all is well and has ever been well. In this way we shall truly be carried to our highest good.

We live in a period of disorder, chaos, decay. It is a period of selfish pursuit of possessions, pleasures, power. In this period, specially, we need the supreme equipment of life, that of self-denial. We need to forsake ourselves and walk the way of sympathy and loving service of the poor and broken ones, realizing that the purpose of life is not to amass wealth and power but to be poured out in compassion to a broken world. We need to breathe out the aspiration so beautifully expressed by the great Buddhist teacher of the Nalanda University, Shanti Deva: -

> *"What is wrong with the world is that we make self*
> *The centre round which life revolves, that we think for*
> *Self and act for self and live for self.*
> *May I cast out this self!*
> *May I be a healer of all beings who suffer and are in pain!*
> *May I dedicate all I am to service and sacrifice!"*

Religion is remembrance. Remember yourself – your true Self. Remembrance, that is to say, collecting again the forgotten parts of man's true Self, is the secret formula for a balanced and peaceful world in harmony with the divine plan.

209

5

THIS TOO SHALL PASS AWAY

It has been said that the only thing that is certain about human life is the fact of mortality: all that is born must die. All that is accumulated must be exhausted. Everything is subject to change and decay here upon this earth.

Contemplating this impermanence is considered to be the best form of meditation. The Buddha has, therefore, said,: "Of all meditation, that on impermanence is the strongest and the most beneficial."

One beneficial result of the understanding of impermanence is that it will inculcate the virtue of detachment in us. If nothing will last, we will realize the futility of clinging on to people, power and possessions. When we cease to cling to these, we learn to avoid unhappiness and anxiety.

If we consider the matter dispassionately, we will realize that most of our problems arise due to our illusions of permanence. We fight, we struggle, we argue over events and situations. Why? Because we believe that these situations are permanent, and that we have to fight in order to change them. If we understand that everything is impermanent, that nothing lasts, we would not act in such a way!

The Universe in which we live, the world of nature around us – everything reminds us of this great concept of impermanence. The vast galaxies, the myriad stars and planets all came into being, evolved, and will disintegrate one day. The succession of the seasons, the passing of time, the revolutions of day and night, the coming of sunshine and rain – everything tells us that change is constant. Nothing is ever motionless in the vastness of space; things are changing all the time! Reflecting upon this motion and this change will help us realize the impermanence at the heart of things.

Let us look at ourselves – the human beings who inhabit this earth. We are all born into this world, we grow old and we die – our lives are rooted in impermanence! Death, when it comes, is the most striking instance of the impermancne of human life.

What are the things we value most in life? Youth, beauty, wealth, power, status, good health, pleasures, family, friends, popularity and fame – none of these can give us protection from death. And when death comes, as it must, all these things will be taken away from us. We cannot take any of it across to "the other side" with us!

Unfortunately, many people consider it depressing and negative to think of death. Some people are afraid even to mention death. Yet others feel frightened and insecure when they hear about the death of their friends or relatives. They do not want to be reminded of what all of us know, but wish to forget!

On the other hand, if we learn to meditate upon death in the right way, we will find that we attain peace of mind. When we face up to the reality that is death, we learn to live our lives more meaningfully.

There is an ancient story told to us about a loving, close-knit family that suddenly lost a grown up son, who was married and had his own children. When the neighbours arrived to offer their condolences, they were taken aback to see that all was calm and quiet and serene about the house. The parents were quietly going about their routine. The wife of the dead man was fetching water from the river, singing God's name as she walked up to the house.

"What is this we see?' said the neighbours, shocked beyond belief. "Why is it that you do not mourn or grieve for the dear departed one?"

Each of the family members had his or her own reply, the gist of which was this: "We know that everything is impermanent. We know too, that, sooner or later, we must all die. Therefore, in the time that is given to us to be together, we try to be as good and kind as we can to each other, and to live in harmony. Our dear one, who has just passed away, never ever said or did anything to hurt us; nor did we hurt him or did him any wrong. Therefore, we have no regrets at all! He has left us, and is following the path of his own karma. This is why we are at peace, and our mourning is serene and quiet!"

The contemplation of death, therefore, need not make us unhappy! Many people who have had a close brush with death – escaped from an accident, or recovered from a near-fatal illness – often tell us that they have learnt to value and appreciate life much more, because they know it is impermanent! When you confront the fact of death unflinchingly, you learn to value life!

Many of us are quite overwhelmed by the petty problems of existence – this man's jealousy, that woman's attitude, the other's rivalry and so on, that we fail to realize the beauty and true worth of human life. When we confront the fact of death, we realize the utter insignificance of these petty problems. We then rise above our lower selves, our binding attachments and our constricting ego. We can learn to become more tolerant, more open-minded, more generous and more understanding. We can learn not to become embroiled in petty arguments, ego-clashes and narrow debates. Above all, we can learn not to let little things disturb us and affect our peace-of-mind. We can learn to take things in our stride and to welcome happiness and unhappiness as God's *prasadam*.

Once upon a time, a great and powerful emperor decided to have a very special jewel-encrusted signet ring made exclusively for his personal wear. On the ring, he wanted to have engraved a few words which would never ever fail to comfort him in times of distress. He offered a huge reward to any one of his subjects who would suggest the best words of wisdom for this purpose. Many people came forward with their suggestions – *slokas, mantras*, proverbs and wise sayings which they valued. None of them appealed to the king.

A Rishi came to visit the palace, in the course of his *yatra*. The King placed his request before the holy man. The Rishi said to him, "O King! Let me share with you the wise words that have always given great comfort and solace to me in times of trials and tribulations. They are just four simple words – *This too shall pass!*"

The words went to the very heart of the King. He had them engraved on his ring: and they never failed to give him courage and faith whenever he read them!

THERE IS NO DEATH

Many of us, I know, are afraid of death. And the very first thought that I would wish to pass on to you today is: Let us not be afraid of death. Death is a natural phenomenon. Moreover death is a very pleasant experience. It is just like going off to sleep.

In a number of messages that have been received from the spirit-world, we are told that the state of death is utterly painless. Before death, a man might have passed through a serious illness, on account of which his body might have experienced great physical pain: but in the few moments before death occurs, all pain ceases, and man has the most pleasant of sensations that he has ever experienced. We are also told that, after death, man continues to be what he was before death. Man remains unchanged. All his characteristics – his thoughts, his emotions, his desires, his memories – are the same: they are unchanged.

A spirit is reported to have said: "We feel the change just as a serpent might feel, perhaps, when it has left the slough." Serpents change their outer coverings which are called slough. The serpent continues to live in a new skin. The serpent is the same; it has only cast off its old skin and worn a new one. That is just what happens to man in death. He puts off his outer body, the physical body.

Man does not die: he only puts off the physical body. In the messages that come to us from the spirit-world, we are told that, when the soul drops its physical body, he can see his friends and relatives, and is greatly pained to see them mourning for him. He tries to explain to them that he has not died, that he is as much alive as anyone of them. He comes and whispers into their ears: "Why do you think I have died? Here am I, as much alive as any of you!" He comes and touches them and tries to comfort them. But because he is no longer in a physical form, he cannot be perceived by his friends and family. Within a few minutes, he realizes the futility of his attempts, as the touch of his astral hands cannot be felt by friends and relatives who wear physical bodies.

Whenever I am called to a place where someone has died, the very first thing that I tell them is this: "Do not weep, do not shed tears, do not grieve over the passing away of your dear one, for he is not dead. He lives in the Life that is undying!" When you indulge in weeping and wailing, you do harm to your dear ones. The more we grieve over them, the more we cling to them, and so become a hindrance in their progress on the Other Side. We must not cling to them, but we must release them, so that in their new journey, they may move on – ever onward, forward, Godward. We should remember them in our prayers and, everyday, we should do some little deeds of service, in their name. This will bless them and help them in their new journey.

Immediately after death, a man looks around him and sees the same house with which he is familiar. He sees his physical body lying in a horizontal position surrounded by those whom he has known and loved, for they also have astral bodies, which are within the range of his new vision. Gradually, he realizes that there is some little difference. He soon finds that he does not feel any pain or fatigue. The astral body does not experience pain or hunger and does not need to sleep. In death, man drops the physical body and continues to live in the astral body. In all other respects, he continues to be the same. His thoughts and desires, his emotions and aspirations and memories are exactly the same as before. He is in every way the same man, minus his physical body.

The physical body is a house in which we dwell for a brief while. The house crumbles: the one who dwells in the house moves on. The body is a cage. You are the bird that dwells within the cage. When the cage breaks, the bird flies away. The body is an instrument through which the soul does its work during its earth-incarnation. The body is an instrument. Therefore, take care of the body. Keep it pure and clean, healthy and strong. Do not neglect the body. Do not throw it in a whirlpool of pleasures. Take care of the body. It is an instrument. If the instrument is in proper condition, you will be able to do your work well.

The body is a boat which is meant to take us to the Other Shore. Therefore, take care of the body, but do not, for a single moment, identify yourself with the body. When the body dies, you do not die. You are deathless. Death cannot touch you. Death can only touch the mortal body.

In ancient India there was a teaching that was passed on to every student. The student was called a *jignasu*, a seeker after truth. And to the *jignasu*, the Rishi, the Teacher said: "My child, everyday, for sometime, meditate on death!" I would wish every one of you to do likewise! The day is coming when this body will drop down – the body of which we make so much, the body of which we are so proud. If we meditate on death, we shall no longer be afraid of death. We shall then know that death is only an illusion, only an appearance. In reality there is no death. We cannot die.

Sadhu Vaswani likened the death of the body to the sunset. He said to us: "Sunset is only an appearance, for what is sunset here is sunrise elsewhere. In reality, the sun never sets. Likewise, there is no death, Death is only an illusion, an appearance. For death here is birth elsewhere."

"What is death?" is the question which we put to Sadhu Vaswani once. And he said: "Death is a bridge!" Yes – death is a bridge between the physical world and the astral world. When death comes, we leave the physical world and pass over the bridge to enter the astral world, which is a better, nobler, richer, more beautiful, more radiant world.

On another occasion, we put the same question to Sadhu Vaswani, "What is death?" And he said: "Death is a door!" Death is a door which leads from one room to another. It was Jesus who said: "In my Father's house are many mansions." One of the mansions is the physical plane, the earth-plane. There are other mansions: there are other worlds. And death opens the door to those other worlds.

John Masefield, the Poet Laureate of England, says in one of his poems: "Death opens unknown doors. It is most grand to die!"

In the new journey on the Other Side, we are not alone. Our dear ones who have passed away, will come and receive us at the railway station, when we arrive at a new place. So it is that you might have found the faces of dying persons light up with radiant joy. Some of them even sit up and stretch out their arms. Some of them call out the names of loved ones who have previously died. Dr. Leslie Weatherhead, who has made a study of this subject, tells us in his book. *After Death*: "I have never seen anyone in any kind of distress at the moment of passing."

Even as birth is the process of taking on a physical body, death is the process of giving up the physical body. The soul immediately finds itself in another body, which has been called the 'etheric double'. What is the etheric double? What is its function? The etheric double is built up of very fine matter, etheric matter. It has the same form as that of the physical body. Therefore it has been called the etheric double.

There are some who are gifted with psychic sight: they have the power of clairvoyance. At the time of a person's death, such people can see the etheric double near the dying man's physical body, and they tell us that the etheric double has the same form as that of the physical body.

Why do we have the etheric double? It is through the etheric double that vitality flows into the physical body and keeps it alive and healthy. That which gives vitality is, in our ancient Sanskrit language, called *prana*. What means this word, *prana*? The word, *prana*, is built up of two words, 'pra' which means 'forth' and 'na' which means 'breath'. *Prana* therefore means 'to breathe forth'.

Prana or the vital force, is absorbed by the etheric double through its specialized equipment, and is dispatched to every part, every cell of the physical body. It is *prana* that makes the eyes to see and the ears to hear and the hands and feet to move. It is *prana* that makes every organ do its work. So long, as the etheric double is in the physical body, the physical body can breathe and live. The moment the etheric double leaves the physical body, it drops down, becomes inert, dead.

The etheric double is connected with the physical body by means of a psychic link which is called "the silver cord." The moment the etheric double leaves the physical body, the physical body drops down dead, but if the silver cord is intact, there is a possibility that the etheric double will once again enter the physical body via the silver cord and the physical body will come to life.

Those that can meditate deeply, hear the music of the silver cord. In meditation, a person gets "out-of-the-body" experiences. Every time that the soul leaves the body and goes to higher regions, the silver cord is struck and its music is heard. The oftener this happens, the richer is the music of the silver cord. In "out-of-the-body" experiences, the soul temporarily leaves the body. In a sense, every such experience is "death" and the great Masters teach their disciples to "die" several times every day. It is only through dying that a man learns the art of true living. The man who has not died, will not know how to live aright.

The silver cord, being of a psychic nature, is not subject to any limitations of a material kind, that is to say, no question arises as to how far it can stretch or extend. There is no limit to its length. The etheric double may get out of the physical sheath and travel many hundreds of miles and return to the physical body, if the silver cord is not snapped. It is only when the silver cord is snapped that the physical body becomes dead.

We are given a very interesting example of this in a book, which was published many years ago. The name of the book is, *Man is a Spirit*, and the name of the author is J. Arthur Hill. In this book, we are told of an ex-artillery man who sat on the ammunition chest of his gun, when it was hit and exploded. The man was thrown into the air and his body fell to the ground.

Though his body fell to the ground, the man felt that he was up in the air, looking down at his body, which lay upon the ground at some distance from him. He seemed to be yet connected with the body by a slender cord of a clear, silvery appearance, and while he looked on, he saw two surgeons examine the body and pass on, remarking he was dead. Presently, the stretcher-bearers came along and found that there was life still in the body. "I came down that silver cord," said the ex-artillery man, "and returned to the old body, although I was blind as a bat and my right arm torn from the shoulder."

Mark his words! So long as the etheric double was outside

the body, he could see. He saw the surgeons, he saw the stretcher-bearers. And he had no feeling of pain. But the moment the etheric double re-entered the physical body, he found, he had become blind and felt the pain, the agony of an arm having been torn from its shoulder.

We have the classic example of Sri Sankaracharya, given to us in the ancient books. Sri Sankaracharya, in a public dispute, was put certain questions, which he could not answer, as the questions concerned the married state, of which he had no experience. He was, as you know, a *bal-brahmachari*. He was, however, not prepared to own defeat. He asked for time. He moved out of his physical body and entered that of a king who had just died. The body of the king suddenly came back to life and those that were around him said: "The king lives! Long live the king!" In the body of the king dwelt the soul of Sri Sankaracharya who, thereby, got the experience of the married state. After some days, he left the king's body and re-entered his own body. So was he able to answer the questions that were put to him.

The etheric double has no function other than that of keeping the physical body alive. The moment you have discarded the physical body, you do not need the etheric double. When the silver cord is snapped, the soul immediately finds itself in the etheric double. In most cases, the passage through the etheric double is instantaneous i.e. the soul need not dwell in the etheric double, but simply passes through it, relinquishing it the moment the physical body is dead. On giving up the etheric double, the soul enters the astral world. The transition into the astral world should be swift and, normally, man must not linger in the etheric double. However, this is not true in the case of those who cling to matter and material objects. Such individuals continue to live in the etheric double, for it is through the etheric double that they can be in contact with the earth and earthly objects.

When a spirit lingers in the etheric double for a long time, it becomes a wandering spirit, a ghost. Therefore, friends, beware! While you live on earth, see that you are not inordinately attached to any thing or form. Speaking unto his dear, devoted disciple, Arjuna, the Master, Sri Krishna, says : "Arjuna, whatever you think of at the time of death, to that you will go!" Remember, friends this is a great law of life: the thought of a man's last moment determines his destiny after death. Therefore, think of God all the time and do your work. Life is so uncertain, you never know when death may come.

The moment you pass out of the etheric double, you will fall into sleep. It is a deep and peaceful sleep, from which you will awaken, in your own place, in the astral world. In the astral world, each man finds his own place. Your place is where the surroundings and conditions reflect the kind of life you have pursued on earth.

In the astral world you go through a process of disentanglement from desires and feelings. In the moment of death, everyone carries with himself certain desires and feelings. During his stay in the astral world, he is gradually disentangled from those desires and feelings. Therefore, the less the number of desires, the shorter is the period of stay in the astral world. Reduce your desires to a minimum. Live a life of simplicity and purity. The man, who has learnt to control his desires, while on the earth, does not have to stay for a long period in the astral world.

The astral world is a vast region. Even as on the earth-plane there are, on the one hand, palaces and beautiful mansions, and on the other hand, there are dirty slums, even so in the astral world, there are different sections. Each man finds his own place in the astral world. The utterly coarsened creature, selfish, cruel, malignant, will find himself, after death, in the lowest and densest regions of the astral world, surrounded by creations of his own desires and cravings. The man, who has lived the right type of life on earth, who has always aspired to the True, the Good, the Beautiful, who has lived a life of service and sacrifice, of love and compassion, will find himself, after death, in lovely beautiful regions in the astral world. In the astral world, each man finds himself surrounded by like-minded persons. He makes the great discovery that thought is all-powerful. He realizes that the mind is creative; it can create anything. Whatever the mind thinks of is immediately created.

Keeping all this in mind, let each day of our earth-life be a day of preparation. Prepare! Prepare! This is the one word which our dear ones on the Other Side wish to say to us. Prepare! Prepare! For they find us chasing things which, to them, are no better than shadow-shapes. They find us running after money, trying to gather lakhs and crores of rupees, not a single paisa of which we will be allowed to carry with us into the Great Beyond! They find us running after pleasures and sense-enjoyments, after name and fame, greatness and power. These are all shadows. So they ask us to open our eyes, to wake up from the slumber of the senses and the mind and prepare for the inevitable journey.

7

YOU ARE NEVER ALONE

There is a magic mantra that we need to repeat to ourselves constantly. Whatever your faith, whatever the nature of your belief, you need to realize the presence of God within you. And you need to turn inward and contact this Divine Presence within you. This contact is vital to our happiness and well-being. Some of us seek this contact in the temple, church or mosque. Others seek this in silent prayer. Wherever and whenever it may be, this communion with god is essential to recharge our spiritual batteries and keep us fit for facing the future.

A moment's vital contact with God can bring you success, comfort, grace, blessing – whatever it is you seek. Doctors tell us that a moment's prayer, "O God I treat, but Thine is the cure!" helps them connect with God, and do what is just right for their patients.

Patients hand their lives over to God in complete surrender – and find themselves miraculously healed. Doctors or patients, all of us must realize that life itself is a form of prayer, and that we never need to be alone – if only we grew in the awareness that God is always with us, within us, watching over us and protecting us with His love and mercy.

If I aim only at the satisfaction of my desires – however noble they be, if I work with a view to win success or the crowd's

applause, if the purpose of my life is to accumulate things and desire pleasure out of them, I shall find not happiness but emptiness. For all these are shadow-shapes which come and go. The true joy of life is not in them but in the will of the Lord who made me and who made all things that He might give me His love through them.

The chief purpose of my life should not be to seek pleasure and possessions, power and authority, success and security, health and wealth, or even knowledge and wisdom, or their opposites, poverty and pain, ignominy and defeat, disease and death. The purpose of my life should be to seek the will of God and to adore it in the incidents and occurrences of life. In all the happenings of life let me learn to say to myself: "This is what God wills for me. In this does He send me His love. In doing as He wills me do, I receive His love and give it back to Him and with it give myself to Him. So may I grow into the likeness of Him who is the Purest of the pure, the Fairest of the fair!"

Not long ago, a sister came to me. Her eyes were touched with tears. She sobbed as she spoke. Her husband whom she loved and who loved her, had decided to travel to a distant land for purposes of business. He did not lack money. God had given him several lakhs of rupees. "He does not need to go so far, leaving me here all alone," she said. "Pray that he may abandon this idea altogether."

My answer might have appeared cruel to her at the time. "I do not pray for this or that to happen," I said to her. "I shall pray that you may grow into an understanding of what God wills for you and that you may co-operate with His will and let it work, uninterrupted, in and through you!"

The day arrived when she bade her husband a tearful goodbye. "You did not do anything for me," she said to me. "You could have helped me if only you had wished to do so!"

I smiled and said to her: "Sister! Do not despair! God fulfills Himself in many ways!"

After a few months she met me again. Her face was wreathed in smiles. She laughed as a little child. "Now I know," she said, "that there is the hand of divine love and wisdom in all that happens. When my husband left, I wept and wept. Then, gradually, it dawned on me that if God had willed my dear one to travel to a far country, it must all be for my good. Indeed, it has proved to be so. My husband's going away has given me many spare hours, and I utilize them in a study of the *Gita* and the *Guru Granth Sahib* and Beloved Dadaji's beautiful books on the *Sant bani* and the lives of saints. I pray and I meditate. I sit in Beloved Dadaji's holy company. I sing God's Name and I serve the children of the poor and the lowly. They love me. I love them. And I feel happy and blest!

This is perfectly true. Our journey through life has been perfectly planned by Infinite Love and Infinite Wisdom. There can be no mistake. Every experience that comes to us is just the right experience occurring at the right time to train us in the right way. So let us accept all that comes to us and not attempt to circumvent anything. Again and again we try to run away from what appears to us as unpleasant experiences. We try to avoid what we regard as difficult situations. We may succeed in keeping them away for the time being but we can never avoid them all the time, for they are indeed, essential to our growth. God means us to face them and so to develop our moral and spiritual muscles. If we avoid an unpleasant experience, it will return to us in due course with redoubled force and we shall be compelled to take up its challenge until we have learnt the lesson it has come to teach us. The best way, therefore, to face difficult situations is to accept them and co-operate with their inner purpose, all the while fixing our mind and heart on Him who has planned for each one of us the glorious liberty that belongs to the children of the Spirit.

He whose refuge is in the Lord lives in the constant awareness of God's presence. Such a man is never alone. Another is always with him, by him, blessing him, guiding him, protecting him, leading him on! He hears His gentle footfalls; he feels the warm pressure of His Hand on his; he hearkens to the voice of his Unseen Friend: and he always feels safe and secure even in the face of danger and death.

I recall a most moving incident in the life of Muhammad, the great Prophet of Islam, whom the world has yet to understand aright. Information has reached him that his life is in danger, that people are out to kill him under cover of the night. It is a dark hour. With tear-touched eyes Muhammad leaves his home and the town of his birth. With him is his faithful friend and follower, Abu Bakr. In hot pursuit of these two devoted servants of God are those who wish to kill Muhammad. They are so many and they are riding strong steeds and in their hands are drawn swords and sharp lances. Abu Bakr sees them from a distance and feels nervous. In the agony of terror, he says to Muhammad: "They are coming: soon will they slay us with their sharp swords. And our bodies will lie on the desert sands to be devoured by the wild animals."

Muhammad is silent: he speaks not a word. In his heart he feels sure that God is with him and no harm can come his way. Nearby is a cave. Muhammad and Abu Bakr hide themselves in its depths. The party of persecutors halt at the mouth of the cave: their leader suspects that Muhammad is hidden inside the cave. Abu Bakr beings to tremble and whispers to Muhammad: "What shall we do now? We are only two and they are so many!" Quietly, answers Muhammad: "Not so, friend! We are not two but three. The third is Allah. And when He is near, we need not fear!"

A miracle has happened. Just after the two fugitives entered the cave and a little before the party of persecutors arrives, a huge spider crawled to the entrance of the cave and wove its web across it. Seeing the web, unbroken and whole, some of the persecutors exclaim: "Muhammad cannot have got into the cave. Don't you see the spider's web covering the entrance? Had anyone got in, the web would have been torn. Let us not waste precious time: let us move on!" Muhammad is saved!

The man who seeks refuge in the Lord is untouched by troubles and tribulations of the world, its wants and woes, its cares and anxieties. He feels light as the smoke of incense which rises higher and higher. He is not earth-bound. His only quest is God. He yearns for God: he talks to God and to God he offers every thought, every word, every little deed of his daily life. He abides in God. And he feels like a child resting in the loving arms of its mother. Dropping all his burdens at the Lotus-feet of the Lord, he is freed from the fever and fret of the world. He moves through life, singing as he goes, singing the deathless song of the Beloved. Of such as he the *Gita* says:

He lives each day.
Looking at the world with quiet eyes,
Living in perfect harmony with all,
Undisturbed, his mind ever at rest!
He neither loveth nor hateth:
He neither grieveth nor desireth:
Renouncing both good and evil.
He accepts all that comes
As the will of the Lord!
Alike is he in cold and heat.
In pleasure, pain,
In censure, praise.
Devoid of all attachment,
His mind is firm in faith,
His heart is full of devotion.
In the shifting scenes

Of this changing world,
He clings to the Lord alone
And in Him finds his shelter true!

8
WHAT IS MEDITATION

We live in a world of allurements and entanglements. The sharp arrows of desire, craving, animal appetite, of passion and pride, of ignorance and anger, of hatred and greed, wound our souls, again and again. Our souls bear the scars of many wounds: they need to be healed. The word "meditation" is derived from the Latin root which means "to heal".

While many regard meditation as a difficult art, in itself it is so simple. Meditation is directing our attention to eternal things and keeping it there for a while. Within every one of us is a realm of peace, power and perfection. Through practice, we can, at will, enter this realm and contact God. When we do so, we become conscious of infinite power, a wondrous peace, and realize that everything is perfect and in its own place.

To know what meditation is, we need to go within ourselves, and, in the words of Sadhu Vaswani, "sink deeper and deeper." No one else can do that for us; we need to do it ourselves. We need to silence the clamour of our unruly minds. We need to strip ourselves of all pride and passion, selfishness, sensuality, and sluggishness of soul. We need to remove veil after veil until we reach the inmost depths and touch the pure white flame.

As a first step, we need to throw the dirt out of our mind. One is as one thinks, taught the great Rishis of ancient India.

Therefore, take care of your thoughts. Often, we pay scant attention to our thoughts. We say, "after all, it was but a thought." But we must never forget that thoughts are forces, thoughts are the building blocks of life. With thoughts we are building the edifice of our own life, building our own future. People blame their stars, their destiny. "Men heap together the mistakes of their lives," said John Oliver Hobbes, "and create a monster they call destiny." Destiny is not a matter of chance: it is a matter of choice.

We are building our own destiny, every day, with the thoughts that we think. A thought, if it is constantly held in the mind, will drive us to action. An action that is repeated creates a habit. It is our habits that form our character. And it is character that determines our destiny.

Like all spiritual experiences, meditation is something that cannot come to us from without. It is true, in the early stages of our spiritual unfolding, the "exterior" life, in a large measure, does shape the "interior" life. What we think and feel, what we read and hear, what we do and speak, is echoed in the hours of silence. So it is that we must take the greatest care of our "outer" life. We must keep sentinel over our thoughts and feelings, our aspirations and desires, and our words and deeds.

Meditation is gazing inward by opening another aperture of the mind. It is turning away from all outer objects to seek Him whom the Rishis call *ekamevaadvityam* – the One without a second, the One and only Reality. Meditation is entering upon the interior pilgrimage in which layer after layer of unreality is to be torn. The pilgrim, therefore, proceeds by negation: *neti, neti,* not this, not this! These are not God: I seek Him alone!

The pilgrim enters, more and more into silence. In silence, he understands the secret of true freedom. In silence he makes the discovery that he is not a creature bounded by space and time. He is a child of Eternity: and Eternity is here and now.

He is not the isolated creature he thought himself to be. He is a "wave of the unbounded deep." He is one with all life, all creation. He is in all: all are in him!

As we sit in silence, let us think of a world that is very much like this world but that is free of all disorder and chaos – a world in which everything is done for love's sake, where everyone readily extends a helping had to everyone else, where everything comes to pass in the right way, at the right time, in a perfectly harmonious manner. As we do this, we will find the perfection and peace of God flowing into our lives like a perennial river.

In the journey to the Uttermost, it is helpful to have the grace and guidance of a Godman or a friend of God – someone who lives and moves and has his being in God. Him we call a Teacher, a Guru. An enlightened one, a Man of Light. Sadhu Vaswani often said to us, that such a man is better than a thousand men who may have read thousands of books. If you would enter into the secret of life – the secret that is God – go and seek someone who is pure and holy and free. Through grace, you will find it easy to tread the Path which the Upanishads have called the "razor's edge". To grow in the inner life, the life of the Spirit, I need to withdraw from the outer world of noise and excitement. Each day, I must spend some time – at least an hour in silence. At the very start, perhaps, it will be difficult to sit in silence for an hour at a stretch. Then it would be well if I practice silence for about a quarter of an hour, four times a day.

Sitting in silence, what do I find? I find that I am overwhelmed by a new type of noise. For noise is of two types: 1) exterior; and 2) interior. It is easy to keep away from outer noise. There are silence spots in every place, where the din and roar of cities do not reach. But it is a difficult task to still the noise that is within – the clamour of conflicting thoughts.

Things and thoughts to which we pay the least attention during waking hours, rise out of nowhere and, like swarms of mosquitoes, disturb our peace. The more we try to brush them aside, the more formidable they become.

What am I to do? Do nothing. Let me but sit still, as a silent spectator viewing the shifting scenes of a fickle mind. Let me but sit as, years ago, I sat in a theatre watching a play. The actors appeared on the stage, played their respective roles, then disappeared: I kept looking on! So, too, let me keep looking on at the thoughts that rush out of the unknown deep in a seemingly endless procession. They are not my thoughts. I have naught to do with them. They come: let them come. They will soon pass out, leaving the chamber of my mind cleaner and brighter than before. They are the dirt and filth that have accumulated within the cells of my mind during a life time, or, maybe, during many long ages. If the dirt and filth are washed off, I have every reason to rejoice. The bad odour that is let out in the process should neither frighten me nor disquiet my mind.

In due course, the mind will become calm and clear as the surface of a lake on a windless day. Such a mind will become a source of indescribable joy and peace. Significant are the words of the Upanishad: "The mind alone is the cause of man's bondage: the mind is, also, an instrument of man's liberation."

To sit in silence, I must learn to be still. To be still, I must learn the art of separating myself from the changing moods of the mind, from its flights, which are faster by far than the fastest supersonic jets.

One simple exercise will be very helpful. Let me imagine the mind in the form of a room. In this room let me select a corner and sweep it clean. Then let me sit in the corner and quietly watch the antics and acrobatics of the mind. If only I can dissociate myself from them, I shall have thrown off the yoke of the mind. I shall have broken the tyranny of the "ego", which is the only hurdle between me and my god: I shall have grown into that true awareness that, in the midst of my daily duties, I can keep my heart fixed on the One Divine Reality.

Yet another exercise can be found very helpful. As I sit in silence, let me offer my mind at the Lotus Feet of the Lord. Every time I find the mind flying off on a tangent, let me quickly and gently bring it back to the Lotus Feet. If, for a whole hour, I have done no more than bring the mind back to the Lotus Feet every time it has moved afar, I have not spent the hour in vain. Gradually, the mind will be tranquilized and I shall taste and know how sweet it is to sit in silence.

Sitting in silence, let me repeat the Divine Name or meditate on some aspect of the divine Reality or on an incident in the life of a man of God. God, it is true, is Nameless: but the sages have called Him by many Names. Choose any Name that appeals to you: repeat It again and again. Repeat the Name – yes, but not merely with the tongue. Repeat It with the heart: repeat It in love and adoration. Repeat It with tears in the eyes. Repeat It until you can repeat It no longer, until you disappear from yourself, your "ego" is dissolved, and you sit in the presence of the Eternal Beloved. I sometimes think of the Name Divine as a locked door. If only we can open it, we, too, may live in the abiding presence of the Beloved. The way to open it is the Way of Love.

We may also meditate on some form of god – on Krishna or Christ, on Buddha or Nanak, on a Saint or a Holy One. God is the Formless One: but, for the sake of His devotees, he has put on many forms and visited the earth. Choose any Form that draws you: meditate on it. There should, however, be no attachment to the Form: all forms, ultimately, have to be left behind. Significant are the words of Eckhart: "He who seeks God under a settled form lays hold of the form, while missing the God concealed in it." Meditate on the Form to which you feel drawn, then go beyond it. Enter into the Form to meet the Formless one!"

The Buddha speaks of five types of meditation. The first is the *meditation of love* in which we so adjust our heart that we wish for the happiness of all living things, including the happiness of our enemies.

The second is the *meditation of compassion*, in which we think of all beings in distress, vividly representing in our imagination their sorrows and anxieties so as to arouse a deep compassion for them within us.

The third is the *meditation of joy*, in which we think of the prosperity of others and rejoice with their rejoicings.

The fourth is the meditation on impurity, in which we think of the evil consequences of immorality and corruption. In this meditation, we realize how trivial is the pleasure of the moment and how fatal are its consequences!

The fifth is the *meditation on serenity*, in which we rise above love and hate, tyranny and oppression, wealth and want, and regard our own fate with impartial calm and perfect tranquility.

Meditation disciplines the mind, sharpens concentration and improves memory. It also energizes body and mind. Thus modern medical practitioners have begun to use it as an effective aid in healing and therapy. Meditation also helps the mind to relate to our inner instinct – intuition. This connection aids our creativity and innovative thinking. Thus meditation is a systematic method of tapping human brilliance.

The life of meditation, however, must be blended with the life of work. We must not give up our worldly duties and obligations in order to meditate. We must withdraw ourselves from the world for a while and give ourselves wholly to God. Then we must return to our daily work, pouring into it the energy of the spirit. Such work will bless the world. Through such work will God Himself descend upon the earth. Work of the true type is a bridge between God and humanity. So with one hand let us cling to His Lotus Feet and with the other attend to our daily duties.

CONCLUSION

This collection would be incomplete without offering a flavour of the relationship between Sadhu Vaswani and Dada Jashan, between *pir* and *murshid*, between *guru* and *shishya*. Therefore as a conclusion we offer you some anecdotes in the words of the disciple. They speak more eloquently than any description by a third person could.

Dada J.P. Vaswani on His Master

"What is God?" I asked him, many years ago, as he sat in the little garden of his house underneath the canopy of the clear, star-lit skies of Sind. A gentle breeze blew, touching our nostrils with the sweet aroma of the *rajani* flower, the "queen of the night". All around was a strange, wondrous silence.

On that beautiful, unforgettable night, Beloved Dadaji spoke to me of several things, of the Kingdom where neither sun nor stars do shine, of the re-birth of man, of the treasures of wisdom, of the beauty of the One Beloved whose vision emancipates the heart, of the love which travels from God to man and back from man to God. And I asked him: "Dadaji! Tell me what is God."

And he said: "God is Truth. And God is Good, Absolute Good. And God is Beauty. And God is Holiness. The human soul has somehow lost Him: and He may not be found again until, in His infinite grace He comes down and touches the human soul. For it is true, too true, that behind man's search for God is God's search for man. God seeks man. God seeks every one of His children who have turned away from Him. And God will not rest until we all have returned to Him. Therein lies our deepest hope."

What is it that stands between man and God?" I asked.

And he said: "Veils have fallen on man: and he remains sunk in ignorance and apathy: he is unable to see God. Man, under the influence of his gross physical environment, is blind to the beauty of God and runs after the vanities of the world. Man is a victim to the one great veil – that of appetite or desire: the flesh is a very serious veil. Desires dominate man and he turns his face away from the Light.

"Man may turn to Him again and behold the beauty of God. This may be achieved by God's mercy and grace. Beholding Him by His grace, we may see Him as Light. Not until the seeker travels to the Realm of Light, may he become truly a man. Most of us are no better than animals – excommunicated from the City of Light. Man, tied to a life of the senses, is no better than a brute-beast. Man's destiny is to be a divine bird – to grow wings and fly from this world of darkness to the radiant world of Light."

"What may I do," I asked him, "to grow wings and fly to the realm of radiance and light?"

And he answered: "Realize, first, that you live in a state of banishment from the Beloved. Then know that you must die to 'selfhood' in order to live in the Beloved."

"What is the path that leadeth to the City of Light, the City of God?" I asked.

He answered: "Many be the paths that lead Godward. The essence of them all is in two things:

"1) When the little self, the 'ego' dies, we enter into the Limitless";

"2) The limitless is Love – the all-living Love. When the Heart is pure, Love glows in the Heart within."

And I asked him: "How should a man prepare to behold the face of Love in the Heart within?"

And he said: "Concentrate on the Heart! It is a mirror in which you may behold the face of Love. But the mirror is soiled, is greased, and the reflection of the Beloved is blurred. Cleanse the mirror of your Heart. Wipe away the impurities which stain the Heart. The one great source of impurities is 'ego', 'self'. When the ego is annihilated, the Face of the Beloved is seen shining in the mirror of the Heart."

And I asked: "How may the 'ego' be annihilated?"

He said: "As the seeker makes progress on the Path, he finds that sometimes he prides himself on his efforts. Sometimes he thinks he is achieving success. Sometimes he loses the joy of existence. It is so difficult, he says, to be spiritual. Then comes to him a realization that his efforts and endeavours are not pure but tainted, spotted. The darkest spot, he finds, is the little 'self', the 'ego' the "I". And he begins to realize that of his own accord he can do nothing. Then he learns to accept whatever comes – abasement, criticism, contumely – as the will of god. Love of God gradually fills him: his "egoism" dies. A higher stage is still to come when he realizes that God loves him and hath awakened love in his heart. Then he realizes that Divine Love and Divine Grace encompass life from beginning to end. Then all desires, appetites, allurements, attachments, depart: he is free: he is calm!"

....

A Pundit, proud of his studies in shastric lore, asked him once: "How far may a study of the *shastras* (scriptures) help a seeker on the Path?"

Dadaji answered: "the *shastras* are often studied as an

intellectual exercise: and not unoften their students quarrel among themselves in regard to the interpretation of the texts. The darkness of a room is not dispelled by uttering the word 'lamp'! So the darkness of the 'ego' is not removed by the word-meaning of the scriptural texts. This darkness will not be dispelled until the 'inner light' is unveiled. And the 'inner light' may be unveiled through the help of an illumined One. Him we call a Guru."

"What is the essential mark of the true Guru?" I asked him, one day.

And he said: "The true Guru is even he who is in communion with the divine Life."

"And how does the true Guru help his disciple?" I asked.

"The Guru tries to transform the pupil," he answered. "The Guru kindles in the heart of the pupil the fire of the Spirit. The pupil is transmuted into the very substance of the Guru. The pupil, like his Guru, shines with the light of Life divine."

"What are the essential marks of a perfect disciple?" I asked. And he said: "The following seven:

"1) He is obedient to his guru.

"2) He is pure-minded: he has risen above the mirage or *maya* of life. He has renounced sexual deformity. He has turned away from all ephemeral pleasures and fleeting sensations.

"3 He is strong in the aspiration to *moksha* (liberation).

"4) He is diligent and devoted to the welfare of others.

"5) He is never tired in the service of the Guru and he serves him by speech and thought, by body and will.

"6) He listens to the voice of silence. He is awake within and he is active on the outer plane. In quiet retreats – on mountain-tops and silent hills, in caves and forests, on river-banks and seashores – he hears the holy vibrations. To the noises around him he is deaf: and even in the market-place he is awake to the notes of the Eternal.

"7) He has conquered his passions – indolence, lust, anger, greed and *moha*."

....

A University professor came to meet him, one day, and in the course of his talk asked: "What are the marks of a man of true knowledge?"

And Dadaji said: "The following five: 1) he is free from impurity; 2) he has peace in his heart, amid the fleeting phenomena of life; 3) he is free from pride; 4) he is a man of illumination; and 5) he is holy."

"What things are necessary for spiritual advancement?" was a question repeatedly asked him.

And he said: "Only two things: 1) realize that all things are transient, all things pass away; and 2) give brotherly love or compassion to all."

"What is the way to emancipation?" was the question put to him by a Buddhist bhikkhu in Sri Lanka.

And Dadaji said: The way is two-fold: 1) meditation – in silence; and 2) compassion, selfless service."

"What is the essence of religion?" he was asked by one of a group of American University students and professors who visited Indian on a "cultural mission".

And Dadaji said: "Know thyself! See the One Life in all creation, and give love to all!"

Thereupon one of the students asked: "What is the way to know myself?" And Dadaji said: "If you will know yourself, lose yourself, in love: and you will find yourself."

I asked him, one day, for a map of daily life. And he

said: "Aspire each day to live a holy life. Therefore, note the following: never speak untruth. Always avoid slander. Heal divisions. Strive for harmony. Be compassionate to all creatures. Shun luxuries, shows, idle talk, vain arguments. Spend sometime in silence and meditation. Abandon incontinence. Live in perfect charity. Sing the Holy Name. And breathe out peace to all beings."

During one of his visits to Bombay, the newspapers spoke of beloved Dadaji as a poet, a mystic, a philosopher. With a twinkle in his eyes, he said to me: They have not understood me. I am none of the things they write about me. I but aspire to be a bhakta, a lover of the Lord."

"What is the way of love?" I asked him.

He said: "The way of love is the little way."

"What is it to tread the little way?"

And he answered: "To tread the little way is to be humble as dust: for the heart must be emptied before it can receive the treasures of the Spirit."

If I were asked to express the secret of his life in a few words, I would sum it up in two words: "humility and love." His humility defied description: and his boundless love moved out alike to the saint and the sinner, to the rich and the poor, to the great and the small, to men in power and to those whom the world tramples upon, every day. Many of those who came in contact with him were wonderstruck at his humility and love. One who met him for the first time, could not help but exclaim: "I have never received such love in all my life! Not even my parents, not even my children, have loved me as Dadaji has done, during the few, brief minutes that I have spent in his soulful company!"

His humility was the humility of one who has reduced himself to naught. The deepest aspiration of his life was to become the "lowest of the low." Destiny had dragged him, again and again, out of his solitude to perform "great" things in life: but he always felt happy in doing little things. Great was his joy when he swept a room belonging to an 'untouchable' and when he washed a beggar's body clean, clothing it in new garments. His face was lit up with joy as he sat at the grinding-stone making flour for feeding the poor. He felt inexpressibly happy when, out of his own hands, he fed the little birds that swarmed in hundreds on the roof of his house, at Karachi.

"What is your ambition?" he was asked by a press-correspondent. And Dadaji said: "I have no ambition. Every ambition is a chain which binds us to the earth. I but aspire to become a little one!"

The emphasis in his life was on being little. "In my hermit-heart," he said, "there sings a little song: "May I be as Thy little ones, the rose, the leaf, the lisping child!" He taught by precept and example that greatness was a malady to be shunned. God asks not for great things he said. Little things were precious to the Lord.

Day after day, Dadaji showed to us, if we will but open our eyes and see – what it is to walk, pilgrim-like, the "little way." Dadaji had become a "little one", pouring out his life as an offering to the "Lord of the poor and little ones." In an age intoxicated with "ambition" and the mad rush for "bigness" Dadaji's life rings with the message: "Pilgrims are ye all! Walk ye the little way!"

Thinking of him and the stainless purity of his life, of his humility and love, of his spirit of detachment blended with compassion, of the flame of divine life that burnt ceaselessly within him, of the smile that played upon his lips and the sadness that lay in the depths of his eyes – the sadness of all the world – I have whispered to myself, again and again:

In all the world there is scarce another like unto thee!

Thou art the mountain-peak: I am a frail climber!
Thou art the ever-loving mother: I am a child
Lost in the fair of this world!
And yet this have I learnt of thee,
That I am thy yesterday, thou art my tomorrow.
I am a tiny stream: thou art the rushing torrent
And if only I flow into thee, together we shall move on
And become one in Him who is the End and
Fulfillment of life!

FULL CIRCLE

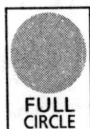

Full Circle publishs books on inspirational subjects, religion, philosophy, and natural health. The objective is to help make an attitudinal shift towards a more peaceful, loving, non-combative, non-threatening, compassionate and healing world.

We continue our commitment towards creating a peaceful and harmonious world and towards rekindling the joyous, divine nature of the human spirit.

Our fine books are available at all leading bookstores across the country and the Full Circle premium bookstores below:

Bookstores

23, Khan Market, 1st & 2nd Floor
New Delhi-110003 Tel: 24655641/2/3

N-16, Greater Kailash Part I Market
New Delhi-110048 Tel: 29245641/3/4

Number 8, Nizamuddin East Market
New Delhi-110013 Tel: 41826124/5

G-27, Sector-18, NOIDA-201301
Tel.: 0120-4308504-7

contact@fullcirclebooks.in
www.fullcirclebooks.in

Enjoy Radiant Health with this Remarkable Handbook!

Join the
World
Wisdom
Book Club

GET THE BEST OF WORLD LITERATURE
IN THE COMFORT OF YOUR HOME AT
FABULOUS DISCOUNTS!

Benefits of the Book Club

Wherever in the world you are, you can receive the best of books at your doorstep.

- Receive FABULOUS DISCOUNTS by mail or at the **FULL CIRCLE** Bookstores in Delhi.
- Receive Exclusive Invitations to attend events being organized by **FULL CIRCLE**.
- Receive a FREE copy of the club newsletter — The World Wisdom Review — every month.
- Get UP TO 10% OFF.

Join Now!

It's simple. Just fill in the coupon overleaf and mail it to us at the address below:

FULL CIRCLE
J-40, Jorbagh Lane, New Delhi-110003
Tel: 24620063, 24621011 • Fax: 24645795
E-mail: contact@fullcirclebooks.in *www.fullcirclebooks.in*

Yes, I would like to be a member of the

World Wisdom Book Club

Name ☐ Mr ☐ Mrs ☐ Ms ....

Mailing Address ....

....

....

City .... Pin...............................

Phone .... Fax............................

E-mail ....

Profession .... D.O.B ....

Areas of Interest ....

....

Mail this form to:
The World Wisdom Book Club
J-40, Jorbagh Lane, New Delhi-110003
Tel: +011- 24620063, 24621011 • Fax: 24645795
E-mail: contact@fullcirclebooks.in

FINDING PEACE OF MIND